The Stage Directions Guide to Working Back Stage

Edited by
Stephen Peithman
Neil Offen

HEINEMANN
Portsmouth, NH

For all those in front of the lights and behind the scenes who understand the magic of theater

HEINEMANN
A division of Reed Elsevier Inc.
361 Hanover Street
Portsmouth, NH 03801–3912
www.heinemanndrama.com

Offices and agents throughout the world

LIBRARY OF CONGRESS CATALOGING-IN-PUBLICATION DATA
The stage directions guide to working back stage / edited by Stephen Peithman, Neil Offen.
     p.   cm.—(Heinemann's Stage directions series)
    ISBN 0-325-00244-4
    1. Theaters—Stage-setting and scenery.   I. Peithman, Stephen.
II. Offen, Neil.   III. Title.   IV. Series.
PN2091.S8 S76   2000
792'.0233—dc21

00-040757

Editor: Lisa A. Barnett
Production: Abigail M. Heim
Cover design: Barbara Werden
Cover photo: Rob Karosis
Manufacturing: Louise Richardson

Printed in the United States of America on acid-free paper

04   03   02   01   00   DA   1   2   3   4   5

Contents

Foreword

*I*t's the iceberg principle. Three-quarters of a production is beneath the surface—or, in this case, behind the scenes. And that's as it should be. The play *is* the thing, after all. Yet what goes on back stage forms the underpinnings of what the audience sees. Every task, every detail must be taken into account to mount a finished production.

With that in mind, we've culled the best articles from *Stage Directions* magazine, published since 1988, to provide both an overview of backstage work and some quite specific how-to pieces on a number of important topics. Here, as in the magazine, we have blended our own knowledge of backstage issues with the expertise of stage managers and technicians in community, regional, academic, and commercial theater.

The Stage Directions Guide to Working Back Stage is organized into nine parts:

- Materials: tips on wood, paint, adhesives, and tapes
- Tools: purchasing and maintaining both manual and electrical tools
- Rope, rigging, and curtains
- Safety: from the scene shop to emergency evacuations
- Theft: how to guard your theater against breaking and entering, and internal theft
- Sets and Lights: from scene shifts to taking a show on the road to creating a lighting emergency kit

■ Props: how to borrow, display, and organize them

■ Strike: dismantling a production can go smoothly and safely—if you're prepared

■ Other Issues: finding backstage help, backstage tours, things that went wrong (and why) and more

Besides the informative articles, throughout the book we've also included "Since You Asked," selections from more than ten years of answers to reader questions, as well as hints and tips from our "Did You Know?" department.

As you read this book, it's important to remember that there is no one right way to organize and manage the back stage. A great deal has to do with the physical layout of the theater, the technical amenities provided, the age of the facility, and even the type of production. An effective and safe back stage relies on an entire tool chest of options; you need to understand those options to meet the needs of a specific situation.

So, whether you are a stage manager, technical director, crew member, or just testing the waters of technical theater, we hope *The Stage Directions Guide to Working Back Stage* provides you with the tools you need to keep things running smoothly.

About Stage Directions

The majority of the material in this book is based on information that first appeared in the pages of *Stage Directions*, the "practical magazine of theater." Since 1988, *Stage Directions* has published articles on a wide variety of subject matter—not only working back stage, but also acting and directing, management, scenic and costume design, lighting and special effects, publicity, and much more.

During that time we've taken a close look at almost every aspect of backstage work. We've put all that advice together in this book, updated and revised as needed, and added introductions that help put the information into perspective.

As we do with our magazine, we'd like to hear your comments on this book, or suggestions for future topics in our expanding library of *Stage Directions* books.

Stephen Peithman
Neil Offen

Introduction

The full realization of the work of director, actors, and designers is dependent on a well-run back stage.

Backstage workers handle a wide range of vital tasks, from move-in to setup to striking the set. These responsibilities involve sets, lighting, sound, costumes, and props, as well as working closely with actors, musicians, and other staff members. And after the production closes, there is maintenance and storage of materials and equipment.

With these responsibilities in mind, this book focuses on how to create a truly collaborative and mutually supportive effort. And because it *is* a collaboration, it is important that you know with whom you are working and what their responsibilities are. You also need to know who reports to whom. This is particularly important if you are new to the theater or if you are providing an orientation to newcomers.

Some theaters have organizational charts, but it's our experience that such charts tend to be the ideal rather than the reality. It's not that people brazenly ignore the organizational setup, but rather that in the press of production deadlines, there is often an overlap as people pitch in to do what is required to get the show on the boards.

Still, even in the most informal of backstage work environments, there must be a division of labor and a hierarchy of responsibility. When decisions must be made or directions given, it's vital that they come from someone with both knowledge and authority.

The easiest way for a newcomer to find out how things work back stage is to talk to people on the staff—paid or volunteer. Theater companies can aid in this process by taking time to brief new workers. The first production meeting is also a good time to review the organizational setup, as well as to adjust the workload to take into account the number of people available to work, their personal preferences and capabilities, and their available time.

Each theater is different, but in general the backstage staff is composed of the following people:

The *stage manager* is responsible for overseeing all the backstage elements of a production, including scheduling rehearsals, making sure actors are in their places, coordinating props and costume usage, coordinating the show start with the house manager, and "calling the show"—signaling light, sound, and scenery change cues. In other words, the stage manager is the one who runs the show from back stage. (Some theaters split the workload between the stage manager and a production stage manager. The stage manager handles rehearsals before turning things over to the production stage manager at the first technical rehearsal.)

The *technical director* (or "TD") is most often the person who translates the work of the scenic designer into a workable set. However, in some educational venues, the TD takes on greater responsibility, including overseeing lighting, sound, the scene shop, makeup crew—and even the stage manager, who is reduced to calling cues.

The *technicians* include the master carpenter, master electrician, and stagehands. They help in the process of turning set and lighting designs into reality. They build set pieces, hang and focus lights, and operate equipment before, during, and after performances. They may be paid or volunteer, but their responsibility is to carry out the directions of the designers, under the guidance of the TD.

In addition, backstage staff work closely with the following people:

The *producer* is charged with obtaining people and materials.

The *director* has the overall vision of the production, interpreting the script through work with designers and actors.

The *actors* deliver the words and actions that the playwright has created, guided by the vision of the director.

The *house manager* supervises the lobby and auditorium.

The *theater manager* is responsible for the physical (and sometimes the financial) operation of the theater itself.

Clearly, there is a great deal—and a great diversity—of backstage activity, and we don't pretend that this book covers them all in detail. However, when you finish reading, you should have a good overview of the backstage world, as well as some specific, practical information that you can put to use in your own work.

So, let's get started.

MATERIALS | PART I

W ood, plastic, metal, glue, and paint are the raw materials of backstage work. Learning to purchase these materials wisely and using them properly will save you money and produce better results.

1 When You Buy Wood

What to Look for and What to Avoid

Shopping for lumber requires planning, decision making and, preferably, a pickup truck. Above all, you need to be able to speak the jargon of the lumberyard, using such terms as *vertical grain*, *plain-saw*, *cups*, *warps*, *checks*, *crooks*, and *bows*. (If you're not conversant, check your local hardware or bookstore for a how-to book with explanations of such terms.) Given the special needs of theater people, we asked some lumberyard experts for their advice, and here's what they told us.

Where to Buy

Different lumberyards specialize in different products, and it's important to know just which. One may specialize in dimensional framing lumber, another in fencing material, and still another in specialty woods for hobbyists. If you need special types of wood, you'll benefit from the expertise of the people who work there. Check the Yellow Pages before you shop.

One important choice facing you is whether to buy from a mass merchandiser, like Home Depot, or from a contractor yard. The yard that specializes in construction lumber usually will beat the mass merchandiser's price on a bid project; consider estimating an entire season's lumber needs and sending your order out for bid to a number of suppliers.

If you're buying only a couple of boards, you can't beat the prices at the mass merchandisers. Conventional lumberyards, on the other hand, sell by the board foot. If you're buying large amounts, compare prices carefully by the board foot between the two types of suppliers. Prices fluctuate constantly as everything from forest fires to imports and exports brings pressure on the lumber economy. Other factors to consider when deciding between a mass merchandiser and a contractor yard are the degree of personal assistance you'll need, whether you'll need to have the lumber delivered, and if there's a charge.

Choosing Wood

Wood has more inconsistencies than manmade materials such as metal and plastic. It's important, therefore, to select wood carefully, since you can't take it back. There are four basic deformities that show up in most wood:

■ *checking*, which means that the board may have splits in it, usually in the ends of the wood

■ *wanes*, where edges of the board are rounded or where bark remains along the edges

■ *warping* and all the related twisting, cupping, and bowing that can occur as wood stabilizes after being cut and milled

■ *knots* and *pitch pockets*

Examine each piece carefully for such defects. For example, pick up one end of a 2×6, turn it on edge, and sight down the length for twists and warping. Bowing is not a problem with lumber that will be nailed down along its length, since it will straighten out once it is nailed down. If the ends are checked, they must be sawed off—meaning that if you need a full 8-foot board, you must purchase a 10-footer. Sap pockets are not a problem unless they are in highly visible places where there may be leakage, which can alter the finish; in this case they must be treated and primed first.

Note that lumber actually comes in only four grades (1, 2, 3, or 4), no matter what else it may be named. Number 1 is the highest quality. For set-building, a lower, cheaper grade is usually fine, since it won't be viewed close up. Green lumber is easier to nail and work with. It will shrink eventually, but in set-building this isn't usually a problem. If you do buy green lumber and don't plan to use all of it on a set, stack it carefully to prevent the boards from twisting out of shape for later use.

If you're concerned about strength, look at the annular rings and note how far apart they are from one another. The farther apart the rings, experts tell us, the faster the tree grew and the less strong it is. Particle-board products are cheap, but should not be used in set construction because they are heavy and lack strength. (For more on this subject, see Part IV, "Backstage Safety.")

Plywood is a versatile wood product. Three-quarter–inch sheets are best for platform flooring, since they bear weight extremely well. One-quarter–inch sheets are best for vertical surfaces. Many theater companies use doorskin for walls; it is very flexible, easy to cut, and relatively inexpensive. It also can be kicked in by a careless actor.

Some Last Words

Before you purchase, prepare a shopping list of the lumber required for your project. List materials by type and the number of each type required; for example: "Douglas fir 2×4-inch by 8-foot; four required."

Sticky Situations
Choose the Right Glue for Solid Success

2

Glue comes in a wide variety of forms—some might say a bewildering variety. To choose the right one, you need to determine the types of materials being glued—wood to wood, metal to glass, ceramic to ceramic, and so on. In the chart on page 8, we've listed the most common types of glue available, their uses, and set-ting/curing time.

Once you have selected the proper glue, follow manufac-turer's instructions. In general, however, observe these seven rules-of-thumb:

1. Start with a clean connection: make sure that both pieces to be joined are free of oil, dirt, and any old glue.

2. If the surface is porous, a single coat of glue will be absorbed with none left on the surface of the joint to form a connection. Use at least two coats.

3. Trying to use glue as a filler for large gaps usually results in a failed joint. In the case of wood, you can use wood shavings, toothpicks, or small scraps to shim a joint to make a tight connection. Then use a clamp (see item 4).

4. Clamping the joint increases the effectiveness of the glue in many cases. Tape may work for some connections, but for serious work, use a furniture clamp.

5. Keep in mind that whenever the temperature drops below 70 degrees, many types of adhesive take a longer time to harden. Most experts recommend that most glue jobs be left to cure overnight.

6. Outdoor adhesives are water-resistant and indoor grades typically are not. However, water-resistant adhesives may not be waterproof. If the joint needs to be waterproof, use contact cement or urethane silicone.

7. Be sure to read the safety instructions on the glue you will be using. Most are not hazardous, but a few are flammable, some will damage certain surfaces, and others will bond fingers together instantly.

GLUE CHART

Adhesive	Uses	Curing
white glue	wood, ceramics, paper	sets in 8 hours, cures in 24 hours
yellow glue	wood, furniture	sets in 20 minutes, cures overnight
construction mastic	tiles, plywood panels, concrete, fabric; water-resistant	sets in 5 to 15 minutes, cures in 24 hours
contact cement	bonds veneers, Styrofoam; waterproof	sets instantly, cures overnight
superglue	plastic, metal, rubber, nonporous ceramic; gel form for wood and other porous materials	sets in 10 to 30 seconds, cures in 30 minutes to 12 hours
epoxy	for most materials and for bonding dissimilar materials, such as metal to wood	sets in 5 minutes to overnight, cures in several days
hot-melt	good for most materials where strength is not important	sets in seconds, cures in minutes
acrylic	wood, metal, glass; waterproof	sets in 5 minutes, cures overnight
styrene butadiene	metal, glass, leather, rubber, and plastics	sets and cures in 1 to 2 days
plastic resin	for very strong bonding in furniture repair	sets in 9 to 13 hours, cures in 24 hours
urethane silicone	for strong but flexible joints between wood and metal or metal and glass; waterproof	sets in 20 minutes, cures in 3 days

Sprays

When you need to glue prop pieces together or affix something light-weight to a set wall—temporarily or permanently—spray glues can be extremely useful. There are several types of such glue available, and the right one to use depends on the type of material you are working with.

Examples include spray adhesives from 3M™, including Super 77™, SprayMent™, and SprayMount™. Super 77 is the most durable and has the greatest strength. It bonds paper, cardboard, fabric, fiberglass, cork, felt, metal, wood, glass, foam, or plastic. It's extremely versatile, too: for permanent bonds, spray and attach pieces while the glue is still wet; for a temporary hold, spray one surface and let it dry, then attach. Super 77 is useful where you want to bond materials with a virtually invisible coat of glue.

SprayMent is a spray rubber cement for art and display purposes. It is best for permanent mounting of pictures, signs, and display elements. Its virtue is that it is easily removed with rubber-cement thinner.

SprayMount is a "temporary" adhesive, used in producing layouts for printing or anywhere you may want to put something up and then remove it. If you have a set piece that needs a sign or something similar on a wall in one scene but not in another, try using Spray-Mount on the back of the cardboard. It can be affixed, pulled up carefully, and reaffixed many times.

While all these adhesives are expensive—$7 to $12 per can—a little goes a long way. You don't need to cover the entire back surface of a sign or photograph, either. Spray only the edges and add a light coating down the center; for close-up work (lobby displays, for example), be sure the back edges are evenly coated to prevent the paper from curling up. Always place items on newspaper before spraying; spray particles spread and can coat the surrounding area. If you are spraying something small, place the item in an open-top cardboard box lined with newspaper, which can be thrown away when it becomes sticky. If you do get carried away, excess spray can be removed with rubber-cement thinner on a rag. The 3M line of spray glues is available from art supply and craft stores.

3 Cover Story
Paint Tips from the Experts

Professional painters have a host of tricks and tips that backstage painters will find useful. Here are some we've learned.

■ Before working with paint and brush, apply hand and face lotion or creamy petroleum jelly to your face, hands, neck, and arms. Paint will be easier to remove when it's time to clean up.

■ The stir sticks given out by paint stores can be improved by drilling a few holes in the paddle end. The holes reduce resistance, making the paint easier to stir, and the movement of the paint through the holes improves the blending process. Make sure to blend the paint thoroughly before use; improperly mixed paint will not adhere as well and will be difficult to color-match later, and might not even dry properly.

■ Be sure to remove masking tape immediately after the paint has dried. If sticky tape becomes a problem, use hot air from a hair dryer to help remove it.

■ To keep paint from spilling over the edge of the can onto the floor, tape a paper plate to the bottom of the can.

■ Try using a hammer and nail to punch holes into the groove in the rim at the top of the paint can. Paint will drain through the holes and into the can instead of over the edge and onto the outside of the can. This also reduces spattering when you hammer the top back on after use.

■ When the job is done and before the lid goes on the can, use a marking pen to indicate how much is left by drawing a line on the side of the can. If you plan to store the paint for some time, write down the date last used, as well as the color and color number.

■ Before putting the lid back on, use plastic wrap as a gasket between the can and the lid to ensure a perfect seal. Don't be afraid to store your paint upside down; doing so makes an airtight seal and allows the paint to last a long time.

Sink Saver

An Easy-to-Make Screen Keeps Paint from Clogging up the Pipes

4

*L*ook at that gunk in the paint sink! You know—where you wash all those brushes after hours of painting sets. Sooner or later, those pieces of half-dried paint and other debris will slow the drainage or clog the plumbing altogether. But there is a way to keep the sink clean: install a cleanable and replaceable screen. Here's how.

First, measure the inside of the sink along the bottom. Use these measurements to make a frame of standard 2×2-inch lumber (actually $1\frac{1}{2}×1\frac{1}{2}$-inch) or 2×4-inch turned on edge. Use long "zip" (i.e., sheetrock) screws to hold the frame together, or flat "L" braces on the surface or inside corners. Staple ordinary household screen-door mesh (available by the foot at hardware stores, and inexpensive) on the upper side of the frame. Most screen-door mesh is nylon or other plastic; you also can use metal screen, which is more durable. Attach a pair of handles to the upper surface so you can place the screen in the sink and remove it easily. For under $5 you have a good way to catch 90 percent of the gunk that comes out of the paint cans, trays, and brushes you wash during and after a set-building period.

You also can build a similar frame to go over one edge of the sink under the faucet. Stretched across the top of the sink, this makes a drying shelf for rollers and brushes after they are washed and rinsed. The sink filter can be wire-brushed clean into a trash can. If the screen gets too choked to be useable, simply pull it off and replace.

Because the frame is wood (and prone to warping), you can lengthen its useable life by removing the entire unit from the sink each day and allowing it to dry overnight. If you want a tighter fit between the frame and the inside of the sink, strips of old garden hose or cut-up sponges can be stapled or screwed to the outer edges of the wooden frame.

5 | *Since You Asked*

For more than ten years, readers at theaters and schools throughout the nation wrote to us with a myriad of questions on almost every conceivable aspect of theater craft. They wanted help, advice, and tips on specific situations that had arisen in their companies and departments. They wanted practical guidance they couldn't find elsewhere, which was what the Stage Directions *department called "The Answer Box" offered them.*

Powdered Pigment, Duct Tape, and Dutching

Q. I teach at a small university. A few years ago, the scene shop was supplied with a lot of powdered pigment to mix for scene painting. Although I worked with a designer during my undergraduate days who used this medium, I knew very little about the material. After reading a few sources about the proper way to mix the paint, I have had some luck in making the proper mixture. However, there are times that the process just doesn't seem to work. Is there some formula for properly mixing powdered pigment? I use white glue as a binder, which seems to work well in most cases. But I'm interested in knowing more about the process. On some occasions the pigment doesn't mix well with the binder and water. I have heard that alcohol helps to break down the clumps. What kind of alcohol is needed and how much?

A. Mix and combine powder pigments while still dry. Only after you get the color you want should you add water. Making sure the size water (thinned binder) is workable and of the correct consistency, add enough of it to the powder pigments to create a paste. Stir slowly, eliminating any lumps. Some pigments do not mix easily with other pigments. A couple of drops of denatured alcohol or methanol added to the mixture may help. Begin adding more size water until the mixture has the approximate consistency of milk. Lift the stir stick out of the bucket of color. If the consistency is right, the liquid should run smoothly from the stick, not in little drops. If you are unsure of the proportions to use to create the finished color, mix a small amount of the dried pigments, noting the percentage used of each. To check for color, paint a test piece of wood or canvas and blow-dry. If the result is good, go ahead and mix the entire batch; otherwise, continue the experiment. Be sure to mix more than enough paint, since it is almost impossible to match the color if you run short. Stir the paint frequently as you use it to keep the color true.

Q. Our theater uses duct tape for various kinds of repairs, like mending curtains temporarily, or taping down cables on the floor so people won't trip, or taping together cables hanging from a light beam. Is this OK? Is there something better for that purpose?

A. Duct tape was meant for sealing cracks in heating ducts, hence its name. But warm air is not hot air, and the tape should not be used where temperatures are high—the adhesive will simply give way. (Recent studies indicate that it's not very good at sealing ducts either.) Even at room temperature, the tape leaves a residue when removed (you can remove it with Goof-Off™, sold in paint stores). That's why duct tape should never be used to mend stage curtains, for example. That same residue can foul electrical cables as well. In fact, most professional theater companies do not allow duct tape to be used for any purpose.

For taping cables together, use gaffer's tape, which is black and cloth-backed. It doesn't gum up cables and doesn't stick to itself when you are trying to tear off a piece. Heat doesn't affect it much; you can use it to tape gels to an instrument, for short runs with low-wattage instruments. In an emergency, some lighting professionals suggest Scotch brand Magic Tape™—the dull kind in the green-plaid box—to tape on a gel. You can use it to temporarily splice two pieces of gel when you don't have enough to fill a frame. Many people prefer gaffers to duct tape for taping cables to the floor because the cloth surface is supposedly more skid-resistant.

Check with your local lighting or electrical dealer for the tape; it's also available from many stage-supply catalogs.

Q. I have never been able to answer the invariable question, "Why is it called dutching?" Do you know?

A. *Dutching* or *dutchmaning* means covering a raw edge or joint with a patch of muslin dipped in glue. The term comes from *dutchman*, an old carpentry term for a block or wedge of wood driven into a gap to hide a faulty or badly made joint. Like *dutch treat*, the term poked gentle fun at the Dutch, who were thought to be overly frugal and unlikely to throw out something that could be mended. From this came the broader meaning of covering any gap or flaw.

6 | *Did You Know?*

*T*he "Did You Know?" department was a prominent feature of *Stage Directions* for the magazine's first decade. Short items about sundry theatrical subjects gleaned from companies across America and from various readings, conversations, and other sources, "Did You Know?" offered an assortment of perspectives. Here are some hints, tricks, and pieces of advice on backstage materials culled from more than ten years of "Did You Know?"

Take It Off

Forget scraping and soaking when price tags, stickers, and decals won't come off equipment or other recently purchased items. Instead, tackle the problem with solvents designed for the job, such as Goof-Off™ or Goo Gone™. They not only lift off stickers (and the gummy residue they leave behind), but also remove crayon scribbles, dried glue, chewing gum, tape, and tar from most objects. (They also remove paint, so don't use on walls.) Both products are sold in hardware and paint stores.

Fasten-ating Tips

Here are two useful suggestions from professional woodworkers.

You can stop splits when nailing wood by staggering the nails along the board's grain. Never drive two nails into the same grain line. Blunting a nail's point by tapping it lightly with a hammer before using it will also lessen the chance of the nail splitting the wood as you nail.

If a screw hole has enlarged so the screw has lost its grip, coat a wooden chopstick with glue and use it to plug the hole. When the glue dries, trim the chopstick flush with the surface and refasten the screw. You can do the same with a wooden matchstick to plug a smaller hole.

Sticky Stuff

Velcro™ has many uses for almost any area of the theater, including props, scenery, costumes, and even displays in the lobby. But did you know that it's available in different widths and in dots of different diameters? Depending on the locality, you may find Velcro at hardware, arts and crafts, or fabric stores.

Can It

Don't pour leftover paint down the drain. It will ruin your plumbing and cause problems for the sewage treatment plant. Instead, save all sawdust from shop projects; stir it into old leftover paint until you have a thick paste. Allow to dry and then toss the cans. (Some localities have regulations about paint disposal in landfills; check with your local trash-collection agency.)

The Size of It

When applying sizing to a new flat, mix just enough paint into the mixture to allow you to see where the sizing has been applied. And whenever a flat has been dented, brush water onto the muslin. This should reactivate the sizing and restretch the muslin.

Shine It On

You can "recharge" glow-in-the-dark tape between acts by using a high-powered flashlight (preferably with a xenon bulb) held an inch or two away from the tape. An even better way—if the curtains are closed—is to use a camera flash unit or strobe.

Put a Lid on It

To pour paint with less mess, clean a lid from a used-up gallon paint can. Punch out a 1×2-inch hole about 1 inch from the edge of the lid, using a metal chisel. Use this lid on the can you're pouring from. When done, replace the original lid and clean the punched lid for the next time.

In the Bag

Consider using plastic trash bags to cover stored equipment. With the help of scissors and tape, you can easily make custom dust covers for anything from computer keyboards and monitors to printers to props to sound equipment. And they're cheap. Never use a plastic cover on hot equipment, however—it may melt.

Got It Covered

If carpeting or carpet padding on stairs or platforms doesn't look right for the period or place, try using sheets of heavy corrugated cardboard stapled in place. The cardboard can be painted or covered with canvas and then painted.

TOOLS

Y ou've got the wood, the metal, the paint. Next, you need the right tools to turn them into sets, props, or storage units, and you need to know how to use them properly.

7 The Price You Pay
What to Look for When Buying Tools

You can't build sets without tools—but what price and quality should you look for? The answer isn't simple; just consider the choices you find at any large building supply store.

These guidelines can help you pick practical tools for your theater projects while keeping your budget firmly in mind. However, your choices depend on the work you want to do, how often you'll use the tools, how expert you are at handling them, and how much you have to spend.

Durability

While it might seem wise to buy the best, in reality the high-priced, long-lasting version often isn't necessary. A good example is the throwaway brush, which is fine for slapping paint on sets and flats. Pay for quality and durability in tools you'll use often—basic ones like a hammer and saw, screwdrivers with comfortable handles, and chisels with steel-capped instead of plastic heads.

Don't get sucked into paying more for the "heavy-duty" versions of tools you use sporadically. If you are in the market for heavy-duty tools that will last many seasons, talk to carpenters or homebuilders in your area. Ask what tools they use, what models they prefer, and which they avoid. These professionals have a vested interest in purchasing the most durable, the easiest to use, and the least likely to need constant maintenance.

Expertise

Skill comes from the hand that holds them, not the tools themselves. One of the problems with buying expensive, professional-quality tools for community theater use is that not everyone can use them with the care and skill they need.

For instance, a high-quality flagged and tipped brush in the hands of an experienced set painter will make the work easier, faster, and better. But in the hands of a rank amateur, the brush is no better than the throwaway. So, if you're a practiced painter looking for a flawless finish, by all means invest in top-quality brushes. But if you have a lot of inexperienced hands working on sets, you may want to pass on such items as top-of-the-line, specially hardened, and costly Forstner drill bits. If you can afford it, consider providing two different types of tools—those for the inexperienced, and a separate set (kept locked away) for those who really know how to use them.

Bells and Whistles

Catalogues and stores are full of wonderful multipurpose tools that seem to be the answers to a set-builder's dream. You may find an exception, but in general, avoid them. It may be handy some night to have a combination drill/screwdriver/air compressor, but tools that do a lot of different jobs tend not to do any one too well.

Some tools are dressed up with paint, often to conceal inferior construction. For example, when metal tools are made by the casting method, air bubbles that weaken the metal form as the molten metal is poured into the mold that shapes the tool. If you've ever had a metal handle snap under pressure, it was probably built this way and not *drop-forged*—a process that removes the air bubbles and makes the tools stronger. When manufacturers take the time and money to drop-forge a tool and machine-grind its surface, you'll find that they generally leave the fine-grained metal unpainted. That can be some assurance of quality.

Price

Since the amount you spend depends on what your budget can stand, it's difficult to offer anything but basic suggestions. Your main concern should be to avoid both the most and least expensive models. Top-priced tools may have more capacity or features than you need, while bottom-priced tools too often have fundamental problems built in and may be too frail even for simple tasks.

Finally, be sure to wield the tool in the store and check its feel and comfort. See whether it seems controllable, too heavy, or too light. It can be difficult to compare tools you can't test on the spot, such as power saws; ask about the store's return policy.

Some tools you can test: levels, for example. Before you buy one, check three or four on the store floor or counter, and stack them on top of each other to catch one whose bubble is out of line with the others—not an uncommon event.

Here are more tips from professionals to help you purchase the right tools for your set-building needs.

Power Tools

Which tool is really the most powerful? On the side of every electrical device is a statement of how much amperage the tool draws. The higher the amperage, the less strain on the motor. You may never need all those amps on a drill, for example, but you can count on the tool to last longer.

Wood Chisels

A good chisel lets you do a great deal of cutting without the help of a hammer or mallet. But the differences between good and not-so-good aren't always easy to spot. In general, the harder the steel, the longer the chisel stays sharp and the more easily it cuts. Chisels made of high-carbon steel also sharpen to a finer edge. Professional woodworkers recommend two brands: Sandveck™ and Stanley's Professional Series™.

Squares

The adjustable tri-square is common, but its moving parts make it difficult to adjust correctly. And its metal edge rusts easily, making the measurements impossible to read. Also, sliding the blade through the base becomes difficult. You'll probably find that an aluminum one-piece tri-square will do just fine. They are lightweight and don't rust.

Measuring Tapes

Look for one that lets you replace the blade, since this is the most easily damaged part. A wide tape is easier to use than a narrower one when measuring long distances (15 to 30 feet). The larger numbers are also easier to read. A good choice for these large jobs is the 1-inch blade. It lets one person measure long distances without need of another person to hold the other end.

All About Hammers | 8

Choosing—and Using— the Right One

Then hammer is the universal tool. While the increasing use of screws and bolts in set construction is favoring crescent wrenches and power tools, the chances are that whatever the job, a hammer will come into play. Hammers come in a variety of forms, however, and it's important to know what each is best suited to accomplish. There are claw hammers, ball-peen hammers, mallets, tack hammers, framing hammers, finish hammers, sledgehammers, rigging axes, and more. And most are available in an assortment of sizes.

The weight of a hammer is important to someone like a carpenter who frequently uses one for hours on end. But even for the average set-builder, weight can play a role. A hammer must be light enough to swing briskly, but heavy enough to provide sufficient force to drive a nail with a minimum number of blows.

For example, most carpenters who assemble wood-frame structures like to drive a 16d (16-penny) nail (about 3 inches long) in one or two blows. Carpenters are careful to get a hammer that is heavy enough to accomplish this, yet light enough to avoid wrist or elbow damage—something that a heavy hammer is known to cause.

Hammers used for framing and siding range from 20 to 28 ounces. Finish hammers weigh between 12 and 20 ounces. The most common hammer is the 16-ounce, curved-claw, finish variety.

A hammer has two component parts: the head (the face and the claw) and the handle. The face is the part that comes in contact with the nail, and there are some important things to consider about it. First, there are two face types: smooth and corrugated. The smooth is designed for finish work, and the corrugated face is for rough framing. It is safer to use the corrugated head because it grips the nail tightly and reduces the chance of bending nails. Unfortunately, the same corrugation that grips the nail also can leave a waffle mark in the surface of the wood.

So for fine work (and no waffle marks) that will show from the audience, the smooth-face version is better. However, there is a trick you should know about this hammer. Even the slightest increase in surface roughness can improve friction and reduce nail-bending. Old-time finish carpenters rub their hammer face on a sidewalk. The concrete removes the shine from the hammer's face and creates enough roughness to reduce nail-bending.

A good finish carpenter also never drives a finish nail all the way in with a hammer; the final blows are struck with a nail punch. The nail is driven below the surface, and the hole is filled with putty or plastic wood. Consider this option with set pieces where the nail head would otherwise be seen.

There are two basic types of claws: curved and straight. The curved claw provides more leverage and makes nail-pulling easier. Also, the curved-claw hammer can be used in tighter spaces than the straight-claw type. The overall length of the head is reduced by the curve of the claw. This can make all the difference in the world if you are installing a 12-inch-deep wall cabinet where back swing is minimal. So why the straight claw? In certain tasks, it is the only type that can be used to remove a nail. However, a curved claw is safer during the back swing than a straight claw.

Most theater technicians agree that a wood handle is best, because much of the shock from the hammer's impact is absorbed by the handle. With a solid-steel handle, most of the shock is absorbed by your wrist, hand, forearm, and elbow. Manufacturers are doing wonders with fiberglass and plastic, but in the opinion of most master carpenters, wood still tops the list.

Hammer Types

As we've noted, hammers come in a variety of weights and lengths. Select one that fits your hand and matches your strength. Hammers also come in a variety of forms for different tasks:

■ Curved-claw hammer: the most familiar of all hammers; used for common and finishing nails

■ Ripping hammer: similar to curved-claw hammer; used for prying boards from floors or walls

■ Tack hammer: holds and drives tacks and brads; used in cabinet work and upholstery

■ Soft-faced hammer: often comes with two faces, both covered with plastic or hard rubber; will not mar surfaces; used for assembling and disassembling wood or metal

■ Ball-peen hammer: has two heads, one with a flat surface used for striking cold chisels and one ball-shaped used for shaping metal

■ Hand-drilling hammer: for spikes, cold chisels, and hardened nails

■ Rubber mallet: used in assembling components (such as cabinetry) where pressure is needed but the surface must be protected from dents; also used for gently pounding out dents in metal

■ Sledgehammer: used for breaking up concrete or driving large spikes

9 | Recharging the Light Brigade

How to Lengthen the Life of Cordless Tools

Cordless power tools have been around for a while, but their popularity in the theater has grown dramatically in the past few years. Thanks to improved battery technology and the advent of powerful lightweight motors, the best cordless units nearly match the power and performance of their counterparts that must be plugged into regular 120-volt AC circuits. They are light, maneuverable, and free from tangling cords, so it's no wonder they seem to be everywhere.

However, not all batteries are created equal, so it's important to know which type you have and how to recharge them properly, so you won't shorten their life—or that of your tools. Most cordless driver drills and circular saws operate on nickel-cadmium batteries (nicads), either individual cells or a battery pack consisting of as many as twenty cells. Each cell in a pack is rated at 1.2 volts—join ten and you have a 12-volt pack. The greater the voltage, the more work the battery can do before it has to be recharged (and the heavier the tool). Battery packs usually last through eight hundred to a thousand charging cycles. Replacement packs generally cost $50 to $80.

The length of time it takes to recharge a battery depends on both its condition and the amperage supplied to the charger. "Trickle chargers" work at very low amperage and may take up to 16 hours to fully recharge a battery back. On the other hand, a fast charger uses much higher amperage and can do the job in as little as 15 minutes. Consider these facts when shopping for a rechargeable tool.

Old Versus New

Cordless tools more than a few years old use an earlier style nicad battery that may suffer what's called *short-memory syn-*

drome. This condition results when you recharge some nicad batteries before they are fully discharged, and they begin retaining their charge for shorter and shorter periods. That's why the instructions on most older tools recommend that you fully discharge a nicad battery before recharging. The most common method is to turn the tool on and let it run until the battery is dead. You also can use this method in an attempt to restore a battery that has developed a short memory: run the tool until the battery is exhausted, recharge, then repeat the cycle several times. If the memory doesn't improve, replace the batteries.

Even though these older nicad batteries can be recharged up to a thousand times before wearing out, undercharging them may shorten their life. In other words, read the instructions and don't remove the battery from the recharger before the recommended amount of time. (Likewise, don't overcharge or store a battery pack or tool in the charger all the time unless the manufacturer's instructions recommend doing so.)

However, it's important to know that the new types of nicad batteries now found in cordless tools can be partially discharged and then recharged without any ill effect. You'll get more life out of one, though, if you recharge it only when the tool starts to feel sluggish. However, don't wait until it stops dead—you can damage the cells if you discharge a battery too deeply. As you'll note, this is very different than with older models.

The newer battery packs should be recharged when they're no longer able to accomplish the task at hand (when there is not enough power to drive more screws). Recharging the battery pack before this point reduces its total work life, and discharging the pack beyond this point can damage it.

Again, it's essential to read the instructions to see which type of battery your tool has and how best to recharge it. If you've lost the instructions, contact the manufacturer or visit its website.

With both old- or new-type nicads, once you've started charging a battery, the charge cycle should not be interrupted. If the pack is removed from the charger and reinserted or if power to the charger is interrupted, the charger starts a new cycle, which again can reduce the life of the pack.

Know the Variables

Most nicad cells that go into cordless-drill battery packs are made by Sanyo, Gates, or Panasonic, and battery cells coming off these production lines are not created equal. Cell capacity varies and they are rated accordingly. Battery packs sold as "high capacity" contain only the highest-rated cells, and the better cells take a charge and hold it longer than lower-rated cells. Regular battery packs include cells with a mixture of ratings depending on the company's standards. Make sure that the kit you buy has the best batteries available.

Note that a battery loses 1 to 3 percent of its charge every day, even if a tool isn't used. A few batteries include a built-in LED readout that tells you how much charge is left at any given moment.

Finally, it's against the law in some states to throw nicad battery packs in the trash. Contact the manufacturer for recycling instructions or call the Portable Rechargeable Battery Association at 800-225-7722. You can locate the nearest drop-off center by visiting the website of the Rechargeable Battery Recycling Corporation [www.rbrc.com]. Simply type in your zip code and a list of nearby centers will be displayed for you.

How to Maintain a Spray Gun

Two Basic Operations Will Save You Grief

A properly maintained spray gun should provide theater companies with years of satisfactory service. Faulty spray patterns can be the result of improperly adjusted or poorly maintained equipment. A spray gun is a precision tool that deserves the same care and attention that you give other tools you own.

To ensure top performance, you must provide two basic types of maintenance, according to the trade magazine *Wood & Wood Products*. First, every day you use the sprayer, make sure it gets a cleaning and light lubrication. Second, give it a complete overhaul after heavy use.

The magazine first explains how *not* to clean a spray gun. Never submerge or soak a spray gun in a container of solvent. Doing so fills the internal air and fluid passageways with contaminants. When you remove the solvent, the contaminants stay behind, ready to plug up the gun's orifices or to be sprayed out, messing up your finished coat of paint. Soaking in solvent also removes the lubrication of the mechanical parts and destroys packings.

So, rather than a complete soaking, simply remove the nozzles and tips and soak these parts by themselves. If soaking is necessary to remove these components, submerge only the affected areas, keeping the spray gun packing and gun inlets out of the solvent.

Air and fluid nozzles, fluid needles, and airless tips should be treated with utmost care while cleaning. Never use anything harder than brass to unplug clogged air-nozzle passageways or holes. Tungsten carbide airless and air-assisted airless tips are very brittle and can break easily. A stiff-bristle brush, soaked with clean solvent, is recommended for cleaning foreign material buildup on those components. Never use ice picks, drills, wire brushes, nails, or pins; these ultimately damage the components beyond repair.

Exterior surfaces of the spray gun should be cleaned with

a clean rag soaked in solvent. Once cleaned and the nozzles or tips are reinserted, proper lubrication is in order. One drop of lightweight oil should be placed on the needle valve where it enters the packing just ahead of the trigger. This nut, more commonly referred to as the *needle packing gland*, should never allow the packing inside to dry out or dissolve. If this occurs, lubricate or replace with a manufacturer's replacement part. A worn packing could allow paint to escape or air to enter the gun, causing the gun to spit. Also, lubricate with oil the trigger screws and air-valve system.

Periodically, lubricate all internal threads and springs with light grease or petroleum jelly. Never use any lubricants that contain silicone; doing so leads to silicone contamination or "fishes."

When a spray gun does not respond to periodic cleaning or lubrication, a complete overhaul is in order. To some, this may seem like a major problem; in reality, this need not be the case. Most spray-gun manufacturers sell repair kits that allow for complete replacement of all serviceable parts. Along with repair kits are part sheets that usually contain vital information for service and adjustment.

Do You Know the Drill? | 11

These Tips Will Help You Operate Safely

A vailable in a wide variety of types and capacities, portable power drills are undoubtedly the most-used power tools in the world—and in the theater, too. Because of their handiness and application to a wide range of jobs, drills often receive very heavy usage. Your safety and the safety of everyone around you demands that you carefully check your drills' capacity limitations and accessory recommendations. You should always read the owner/operator's manual as well.

The Power Tool Institute, an industry trade group, also recommends eighteen safety tips to help make sure your power drill is operated safely:

■ Always wear safety goggles or safety glasses with side shields that comply with the current national standard. Use a full-face mask when needed.

■ Wear hearing protection during extended periods of operation and a dust mask in dusty work conditions.

■ When using a drill, do not wear gloves, loose clothing, jewelry, or any dangling objects, including long hair, that may catch in rotating parts or accessories.

■ Be sure the trigger switch works properly. It should turn the tool on and return to the off position after release. If it's equipped with a lock-on, be sure it releases freely.

■ Check carefully for loose power-cord connections and fraying or damage to the cord. Replace damaged tool and extension cords immediately.

■ Be sure the chuck is tightly secured to the spindle. This is especially important on reversible drills.

■ Tighten the drill bit securely as prescribed by the owner/operator's manual. The chuck key must be removed from the chuck before starting the drill. A flying key can be an injury-inflicting missile.

■ If part of the tool, check auxiliary handles; be sure they are securely installed. Always use the auxiliary drill handle when provided (this usually sticks out from the top of the drill case). It gives you more control of the drill, especially if stalled conditions occur. Grasp the drill firmly by insulated surfaces.

■ Always hold or brace the tool securely. Brace against stationary objects for maximum control. If drilling in a clockwise (forward) direction, brace the drill to prevent a counter-clockwise reaction.

■ Don't force a drill—apply enough pressure to keep the bit cutting smoothly. If the drill slows down, relieve the pressure. Forcing the drill can cause the motor to overheat, damage the bit, and reduce your control.

■ If the drill binds in the work, release the trigger immediately. Unplug the drill from the power source and then remove the bit from what you're working on. If you suspect the drill operation you are performing may bind, never use the "lock-on" switch.

■ Never attempt to free a jammed bit by starting and stopping the drill.

■ As you approach hole breakthrough, grip or brace the drill firmly, reduce pressure, and allow the bit to pass through the hole easily.

■ Always have firm footing when drilling. Brace or position yourself very carefully when working on ladders and scaffolding. Be sure of your balance and control before you start the job.

■ Unplug the tool before changing bits, accessories, or attachments.

■ When drilling blindly (you can't see behind what is being cut), be sure that hidden electrical wiring or water pipes are not in the path of the cut. If wires are present, they must be avoided or disconnected at the power source by a qualified person to prevent the possibility of lethal shock or fire. Water pipes should be drained and capped. Always hold the tool by the insulated grasping surfaces, if provided.

■ Remove materials or debris from the area that might be ignited by hot chips.

■ Unplug the drill immediately after use and store in a dry place.

Did You Know? | *12*

*T*en year's worth of tips on tools.

Drill Bit Tip

Plastic tends to chip when drilled with standard twist bits. To avoid this problem, buy a specially ground bit from a plastics supplier, or try rounding the tip of a standard twist bit by slowly blunting its two cutting edges on a grinder. Before drilling, clamp the plastic in place with a backing of scrap wood.

On Edge

Dull tools are dangerous and inefficient. Save time and money by learning how to sharpen the blades of simple hand tools like chisels, planes, knives, and shears. However, let a professional sharpen tools that have complex or contoured cutting edges, such as router and drill bits, handsaws, and circular saw blades. Similarly, leave tools with hardened (carbide-tip and diamond-coated) surfaces to the pros.

Blade-Cleaning Tip

Sawing a lot of pine causes pitch and resin to build up on saw blades, making even sharp teeth seem dull. To clean a blade, spray it with oven cleaner. For easy application, suspend a circular blade on a dowel and hang it inside a cardboard box. Close the flaps of the box for 10 to 20 minutes to localize the fumes, then take out the blade and wash it off with soap and warm water. Dry it thoroughly and spray it with a lubricant to protect it from corrosion.

Some Like It Hot

Some soldering guns come with a cutting tip that lets you cut plastics such as acrylic, vinyl, and expanded polystyrene. To determine how fast to move the tip and how much pressure to apply, first practice on scrap material.

Wax Tape

A steel rule or tape measure gives an accurate measurement and retracts at the press of a button. To protect the numbers and keep the action smooth, coat the tape with a little paste wax, then buff it thoroughly with a cloth.

Taking Notes

You'll always have a place to jot down measurements if you stick a self-adhesive label to the side of your tape measure. Either replace the label when you're done, or erase the marks and reuse it. (However, don't leave the label on for more than a day, or it may be difficult to remove.)

A Point of Light

Create a mini-light for small jobs in tight places by plugging a night-light into a household extension cord. You'll be able to move this little light as far as the cord will reach. When finished, you can disassemble the pieces in a flash.

ROPE, RIGGING, AND CURTAINS

Rigging refers to the complete system of ropes, blocks, and other elements used to manipulate scenery, drops, and curtains. It is the backbone of the theater stage, and therefore must not only handle the demands of the production, but do so without jeopardizing the safety of those who work on stage and behind the scenes.

Rope is used in rigging, but also to lash sets, tie up drapes, and many other uses. Drapes take the form of *teasers* (side drapes or blacks) and *tormentors* (horizontal drapes that block the audience's view of the lighting grid), as well as *travelers* and main (proscenium) drapes. Using and maintaining all these elements is vital—for the success of the production, the efficiency of backstage operations, and the safety of everyone working back stage.

13 | On the Right Track

Proper Rigging Makes Your Curtain Open Smoothly—Here's How to Do It Right

BILL SAPSIS

Stage-curtain track, or traveler track, has been mystifying people since its invention. I've seen track rigged wrong a hundred different ways, but I seldom see it rigged correctly. What follows will explain how to do it right.

Let's begin with the basic styles of track—square-steel type and aluminum I-beam type. Everything else is a variation on these two.

There are two sizes of square-type track and they are used mostly when curtains are doing straight runs. The larger of the two is heavy duty and cannot be curved. The smaller-sized track is for medium- and light-weight curtains and—while I've been told it's possible—I've never seen one curved successfully. The sides of the track will either twist or collapse, making it impossible for the carriers to pass through.

The I-beam aluminum track also comes in two sizes and is used primarily for "walk-along" systems (that is, no ropes, just grab the curtains and pull) or when you need the track curved. A good use of the aluminum track is for a wraparound cyclorama on a black box stage, or in a television studio. Again, the size of the track determines the size of the curtains it can carry.

Now for the hardware:

Live-End Pulley. ■ A track requires two sets of overhead pulley mechanisms. The live-end pulley is located directly over the operator's head and requires two pulleys: one to take the rope away from you, and the other to bring it back to you.

Dead-End Pulley. ■ This pulley is located at the opposite overhead end of the track; it turns the rope around and sends it back toward you.

Master Carrier. ■ The master carrier is the lead trolley (or carrier) to which the onstage edge of the curtain is attached. It's called the master because the operating rope also is attached to it.

Single Carriers. ■ These are the individual trolleys that follow the master carrier. They are not attached to the operating rope; their function is to support the curtain. The curtain has hooks that attach it to the carriers. The hooks are usually 12 inches apart and run the full width of the curtain.

Operating Rope. ■ This is the rope you pull to make the curtain open and close. When rigged correctly it forms a loop, with both sides of the loop coming down from the live-end pulley. Pull one side of the rope and the curtain opens; pull the other side and it closes. The rope is usually made of half-inch cotton with a fiberglass core. The cotton makes it easy to grip and the fiberglass reduces cotton's tendency to stretch.

Floor Sheave. ■ This is the pulley that attaches to the floor, anchoring the rope so you can pull it without twisting. It also returns the rope back up to the live-end pulley and is adjustable so you can take some slack out of the rope when it stretches.

Rig It Right

Now that you understand the track-and-pulley system, here's how to rig a bi-parting (opens in the middle) style track. Start with both master carriers pulled as far to the middle as possible without hitting the end stops on the track. Estimate how long your rope needs to be overall (width of the track plus height times 2), add 10 feet, and then cut it. Take one end of the operating rope and tie it to the stage-right side of the #1 master carrier. Pull the rope stage right, through the live-end pulley, down to the floor sheave below, and back up to the live-end pulley. The rope then goes across the stage, through the #2 master carrier, into the dead-end pulley and back out through the front.

Now bring the rope back across the stage to the #1 master carrier. There, after you pull out all the slack, tie the rope to the stage-left side of the #1 master carrier. Using the attachment devices provided by the manufacturer with the master carriers, attach the rope to the #2 master carrier. You should not cut the rope here. Open and close the curtain two or three times to get some of the stretch out of the rope. Then adjust the tension at the master carrier and cut the rope. This method works for all the different tracks on the market today.

Note that some single carriers (depending on the style and the manufacturer) have holes in them for the operating rope to pass through. The holes look like little tunnels. If yours are like this, pass the rope through the holes.

Needless to day, these are the very basics of track hardware and rigging. They will serve you well in general, but different equipment and mechanisms will require slightly different approaches. Before attempting to install curtain track, call the dealer who sold you the track or the manufacturer who made it. Either of them should have written descriptions of the equipment you are using and/or sketches to show you exactly how it goes together. After all, you've invested a lot of money in this rigging; you want it to serve your needs well for many years to come.

Learning the Ropes

14

What You Need to Know About the New Synthetic Varieties

BILL SAPSIS

Rope is used everywhere back stage, from moving scenery around (and keeping it still) to making Peter Pan fly. But even after several centuries, the composition of rope and its many applications are often misunderstood. In recent years, this has been compounded by the appearance of rope made with new materials.

Rope used to be simple. There weren't a lot of styles and colors from which to choose. There was hemp—what theater people call manila. It is made from dried plants woven together and, because it's organic, it doesn't last forever. In fact, it can wear out or rot pretty quickly, especially if it gets wet. Over the years we have learned—the hard way, of course— that the operating life of hemp in a *normal* working theater is about seven years.

You still will find hemp being used in theaters, but that's changing. New synthetic ropes are coming onto the market that work better and last longer than hemp. But now there are more choices to make. Should you buy a single braid or a double braid? How about a three-strand rope? What material should be used?

Here's what you should know about rope.

Four Basic Types

There are four basic types of synthetic rope on the market today suitable for use in the theater. They all have the same basic properties because they are all made from the same base fiber: polyester.

They all feel good to the hand, being smoother and less

likely to leave splinters in your palm. They all knot well and are extremely resistant to abrasion. The differences can be seen in their construction and respective working load limits. (Keep in mind that these ropes were not designed for the theater. But, then, practically nothing is designed for the theater business; we borrow almost everything from other industries.)

DOUBLE BRAID

The first type of rope, the double braid, is actually two ropes in one. There is a core, which is braided, and a sleeve, also braided. This type of construction makes for a great all-purpose rope. It is extremely flexible and very strong. The working load limit (WLL) of ¾-inch diameter is 2,650 pounds. In addition, it's sold with just about any tracer color you want run through it. (A *tracer* is a colored yarn running through the rope. This is great for those times when you need to identify a single rope in a large bundle of lines.)

Not for Counterweights. ■ However, because this rope is a double braid, a trim mark cannot be run through it without damaging the core. And the sleeve, which is not actually attached to the core, has a tendency to slide over it. These two characteristics make the use of a double-braided rope as a counterweight purchase line a very bad idea. But it is very good for use in a rope (formerly called hemp) house, and it really is ideal for use in block-and-tackle assembly.

SINGLE BRAID

Next is the single braid. It is made of strands of rope braided together. There is no center core to the rope, nor is it hollow—just the braid made from twelve strands of polyester. The single braids are among the strongest of the ropes used in our industry: depending on exactly which synthetic it's made of, the WWL of ¾-inch diameter single braid is 4,800 pounds. It's also easy to run a trim mark (spike) through the braid, just as you would with hemp. And because it does not have a separate core or sleeve (as with double braid), there's no sliding of the rope when you pull on it. This kind of rope is used almost exclusively for purchase (raising and lowering) lines in counterweight systems. It's not used as a general-duty rope because it's more expensive than other styles.

DOUBLE CONSTRUCTION

Another rope used for counterweight purchase lines is the double-construction type. This has a core of parallel fibers and a braided sleeve. The sleeve protects the core from damage. Again, the rope is made from polyester fibers and is extremely strong. The WLL is 2,514 pounds. Because of the parallel core, it has the added advantage of very low stretch qualities. This rope is stiffer than single braid, giving you a great grip. The downside of this type is that you cannot run a trim mark through the rope without damaging it. It is also among the more expensive types of rope.

THREE-STRAND COMPOSITE

The fourth type used for purchase lines is the three-strand composite rope, which is made of polyester and has a polyolefin core. (Polyolefin is a class that includes both polypropylene and polyethylene.) It is, as the name implies, three strands of rope twisted around so that it looks and feels more like hemp than any of the other synthetics. Like the single braid, it's easy to run a trim mark. Because of the construction, the rope will not slide around the core. It costs a little less than the other ropes.

The only drawback to the three-strand rope is the working load limit. At ¾-inch diameter, this rope has a WLL of 1,350 pounds. Remember that when you tie a knot in the rope, you lower the WLL by as much as 50 percent. This means that in a counterweight set, after you have tied the rope to the arbor, the WLL of the three-strand rope can be as low as 675 pounds. So you may have to pay closer attention to your loads.

The choices, then, are fairly simple: for a counterweight set, use a single braid, a three-strand, or a parallel core rope, depending on the strength requirements and your budget. For all your other rope needs, use the double braid.

15 Don't Just Leave Them Hanging
How to Keep Curtains Looking Good

S tage curtains and drapes are costly to purchase and replace, so it's surprising how little thought some theater companies give to preserving them. Here are some care suggestions offered by Syracuse Scenery and Stage Lighting Co. of Liverpool, New York.

First, inspect stage curtains routinely for rips and tears. If repairs are necessary, use a heavy-duty sewing machine or good hand-stitching. Never use tape; it leaves a residue that can never be removed. If tape is used on pile fabric, removal will pull threads from the face of the fabric.

Check to make sure that curtains do not drag on the floor. Pulling a chain-filled bottom hem over a floor area will quickly destroy the curtain.

Curtains that have been treated with a flame retardant should not come into contact with water or other liquids. Water removes the flame retardant and the curtain will dry with a chalky white stain. Such stains don't usually come out; however, if minor water spots are dried quickly with a hair dryer or other mild heat, the stain will not be as great.

When you store drapes, make sure they are neatly folded seam-to-seam and then rolled. This reduces wrinkling. Wrinkles cannot be removed by steaming, since this causes water stains. According to Syracuse, the only safe way to remove wrinkles is to hang the curtain, providing additional bottom weight if practical, and then wait. A general rule-of-thumb is that it will take the wrinkles twice as long to hang out as it took them to develop.

Stage curtains should be dry-cleaned every five years. Like other fabrics, drapes will last longer if they are free of dust and dirt. Your local theatrical supply house may have the name of a reliable cleaner who can take large jobs; otherwise, check your Yellow Pages under "Drapery Cleaners."

Since You Asked

When Curtains Are in Need of Repair

Q. Do you know any way to repair a nearly 2-foot long, L-shaped gash in a velour curtain? It's starting to spread, and mending it with gaffer's tape across the back just pulls out the nap from the welt. Any ideas?

A. The best method is to have the curtain professionally repaired. However, if that's impractical, try this suggestion from Bobby Ann Loper, manager of the costume studio at the University of South Florida.

You'll need an experienced seamster, plus needle, thread, some fabric of the same color (but not as heavy) to patch with, and good light on the work space, Loper says. Position the torn area on a large table, making sure that the weight of the curtain itself doesn't pull on the tear. The surrounding fabric first needs to be reinforced with some darning stitches from the back side. Then carefully bring the edges of the tear together and sew back and forth across it, making sure the thread goes through the reinforced area of the back side in order to keep the two edges abutting. Do not stitch across the front side of the fabric—it will show.

Now, using the lighter-weight fabric, make a patch to cover the area of the tear plus several inches around it. Hand- or machine-sew the patch onto the back side of the curtain and make a couple of lines of stitches $\frac{1}{2}$ and $\frac{3}{4}$ inch away from the torn edges. If the edges still seem prominent, use a hand blanket stitch or a large machine zigzag to hold them to the patch.

Loper says it's better to hand-sew as much as possible because machine sewing crushes the nap on velvet, which might be visible from the audience. Successful restoration depends on where the tear is, how heavy the fabric, and how old, she says. If the fabric is too old, the stitching will just make more places for it to tear. Then it's time for a new curtain.

If you decide to do this yourself, Loper advises, get a sewing book that shows these hand stitches and invest $2 in a quilter's leather thimble.

17 | *Did You Know?*

Safety Cables

Every theater should have a safety cable for each lighting instrument in its inventory. Many come with one when purchased, but older instruments need to have one as well. The standard silver cables are most common, but they also come in black for studio theaters or other intimate spaces. Check your local theatrical supply dealer.

Beware of Knots

Don't let knots develop in rope used for rigging—they can produce bends that reduce the rope's strength. Tests show that a rope will fail next to the knot rather than in the knot itself. The worst offender is the simple overhand knot, which sometimes appears on its own. Because it produces a sharp bend, it can reduce the rope's breaking strength by more than 50 percent. If you leave it and stress is applied to the rope, a permanent weak spot can develop.

Cheap Fix

If you need something on which to hang lengths of cable, hose, or rope, try an old car wheel rim mounted on a wall. Be sure to clean it well first.

Into the Fray

Because they are repeatedly tied and untied, the ends of lash lines often become frayed. If you use cotton lines, dip the ends into white glue and press them firmly into a compact shape. If you use nylon or polyester rope, seal the ends by melting them slightly in the flame of a pocket lighter. Allow the rope to cool before using.

BACKSTAGE SAFETY

*M*aterials and tools, of course, always need to be handled safely. But, in general, working back stage in confined spaces, often in dim (or no) light, with odd-shaped set pieces, furniture, props, tools, and equipment in often unexpected places is a perfect breeding ground for accidents. Even the best-lighted scene shop presents its share of hazards. To prevent injury to both people and productions, all it takes is common sense, an understanding of basic safety issues, and a plan of action.

18 | First, Change the Attitudes

Safety Is a Matter of Planning—and Commitment

E<small>LBIN</small> C<small>LEVELAND</small>

S afety in the theater need not require a huge outlay of time or money. In fact, studies show the most effective way to improve safety is to change attitudes. That's because accidents are almost always the result of a don't-care mindset.

Supervisors concerned about workers' welfare, and who openly demonstrate that concern, are much more successful at changing attitudes than those who "command" adherence to arbitrary rules and practices. The supervisor also must demonstrate respect for the rules and practices. No one will give real support to any regulations if they see "the boss" ignoring those same rules. If you want people to behave safely, do so yourself.

That's rule one. Here are sixteen other simple, cost-free ways to encourage the changes in attitude you seek.

1. *Make safety rules clear.* Use short, succinct sentences with active verbs that make a concise statement. For example, "Wear face protection" is much more helpful than "Be safe out there."

2. *Provide all new workers (or students) with a copy of the standard rules and procedures and be sure they read them.* Make the last page of the document removable with a statement that indicates the new person was given a personal copy on a certain date, and that he or she read it and agrees to abide by the rules. Include the supervisor's name. This mutually signed "contract" immediately reinforces the safety issue in the mind of the new worker. It also can be the basis for future discipline or dismissal, if necessary. (It also might serve as some protection in case of lawsuit.)

3. *Make the penalty for failing to obey safety rules clear.* Then follow up rigorously. Most manufacturing companies follow a three-step system. The first infraction brings a friendly but firm verbal admonishment and a reminder to do better. This exchange is recorded by the supervisor. The second infraction calls for a brief written response with a stronger admonition citing the first infraction and stating the standard penalty if a third instance occurs. Depending on the seriousness of the incident, some penalty may be imposed at this point. A third infraction indicates a pattern of unsafe behavior and may result in dismissal.

4. *Post all safety rules prominently where they cannot be missed.* Good locations include at the call board, the sign-in board, the stage manager's station, and the dressing rooms and lounges.

5. *Place specific safety reminders at each work station.* Many safety supply companies provide low cost, self-adhesive warning labels that can be mounted on power tools or equipment. If you can't afford that, make your own copies on colored paper and affix them with wide transparent packaging tape.

6. *Make the use of safety gear easy and convenient.* If certain tools require the use of safety accessories such as push pads, provide a storage space for them right by the tools—*not* in the tool room. Do the same for safety gear such as face masks.

7. *Use clever or attractive posters as friendly but constant reminders of proper behavior.* Many companies provide such posters as free promotionals. Low-cost ones also are available from safety supply companies.

8. *Make safety equipment prominent* as a visual reminder and to facilitate its use when needed. For example, paint all equipment adjustment controls bright yellow. Paint on/off and emergency stop controls bright red. Place fire extinguishers on a bright red panel with a "Fire Extinguisher" sign above. Use a similar system for first-aid stations, eye-wash stations, and emergency oxygen.

9. *Supervisors should personalize their own safety gear in an attractive way.* That shows others your respect and concern for safety even when the gear is only hanging in your office. A shabby scribble with a felt-tip marker will not have the same effect. Gently encourage workers to do the same high-quality identification of their gloves, hardhats, and so on.

10. *Create safety zones.* These should be around each stationary power tool to prevent accumulation of debris and to remind workers not operating the machine to stand clear. This can be done by

painting a safety perimeter on the floor or using floor-marking tape available from any safety supply house. These safety zones also serve as another reminder for safe behavior around the tools.

11. *Insist on formal training sessions for each new worker.* No one should operate a power tool or a piece of stage machinery without prior instruction and teaching.

12. *Don't allow hazards or misbehavior to exist or persist.* If an accident occurs, deal with the consequences first and then immediately attend to the cause. Workers will recognize this corrective action and safety attitudes will be reinforced.

13. *Clip and post newspaper and magazine articles about accidents and safety.* These are reminders that serious accidents can happen anywhere unless each and every worker makes safety first.

14. *Encourage everyone to make safety suggestions* and respond favorably when they do. Those working in a particular area often are the first to notice a problem there and often have the best suggestions for corrective action.

15. *Schedule regular safety meetings.* You can use free safety films or videos from your library or safety office to inform and instruct. Don't just set up a screening. Plan the viewing and hold a discussion afterward regarding your own workplace and how it can be improved.

16. *Correct misbehavior in a positive way.* First, state your concern for the person's safety. Explain that you don't want anyone injured and you can't afford to lose their valuable contribution to the theater because of a foolish accident. Only refer to company rules at the end of your talk. This method reinforces someone's sense of personal worth and value to the company. Demanding adherence to "the rules" often produces the opposite result and may encourage resentment.

And don't forget to behave safely yourself. Nothing encourages proper behavior like a good role model.

Where's the Fire? *19*
Using and Maintaining Fire Extinguishers

F ire extinguishers back stage are not only a good idea—they're the law. But not everyone who works back stage understands the nature of fire, let alone how extinguishers work or how to maintain them.

There are four things that must exist at the same time in order to produce fire: (1) enough oxygen to sustain combustion; (2) enough heat to raise the material to its ignition temperature; (3) some sort of fuel or combustible material; and (4) the chemical, exothermic reaction that is fire. Oxygen, heat, and fuel are frequently referred to as the "fire triangle." Take any of these things away, and a fire won't start or will be extinguished.

Thus, fire extinguishers put out fire by taking away one or more elements of the fire triangle. Sounds simple, doesn't it? However, not all fuels are the same, and if you use the wrong type of fire extinguisher on a particular fuel, you can make matters worse. Therefore, it is important also to understand the four different classifications of fuel:

■ *Class A*: wood, paper, cloth, trash, plastics—solid combustible materials that are not metals

■ *Class B*: flammable liquids, such as gasoline, oil, grease, paint thinner, and acetone

■ *Class C*: electrical—energized electrical equipment; as long as it's plugged in, it is considered a Class C fire

■ *Class D*: metals such as potassium, sodium, aluminum, or magnesium, almost never found outside of a lab or certain industries (it's unlikely you'll have to deal with a Class D fire, which take special extinguishing agents [Metal-X, foam] to extinguish)

Rules for Fighting Fires

Fire can be very dangerous and you need to be certain you will not endanger yourself or others when attempting to put out a fire. For this reason, when a fire is discovered, first help any person in immediate danger to safety, if it can be accomplished without risk to yourself. Then, activate the building fire-alarm system or notify the fire department by dialing 911 (or designating someone else to notify them for you). When you activate the building fire-alarm system, it should notify the fire department and get help on the way. It will also sound the building alarms to notify other occupants, and it will shut down the air-handling units to prevent the spread of smoke throughout the building.

Only after having done these two things—and if the fire is a small one—you may attempt to use an extinguisher to put it out. However, before deciding to fight the fire, keep these rules in mind. Never fight a fire if:

- *You don't know what is burning.* If you don't know, you won't know what type of extinguisher to use. Even if you have a standard ABC extinguisher, there may be something in the fire that could explode or produce highly toxic smoke. Chances are, you will know what's burning or at least have a pretty good idea. However, if you don't, let the fire department handle it.

- *The fire is spreading rapidly beyond the spot where it began.* The time to use an extinguisher is in the beginning stages of a fire. If the fire is already spreading quickly, it is best to evacuate the building, closing doors and windows behind you as you leave.

- *You don't have adequate or appropriate equipment.* Without the correct type or size of extinguisher, it is best not to try to fight the fire.

- *You might inhale toxic smoke.* If the fire is producing large amounts of smoke you would have to breathe in order to fight the blaze, it is best not to try. Any sort of combustion will produce some amount of carbon monoxide, but when synthetic materials such as the nylon in carpeting or foam padding burn, they can produce highly toxic gases such as hydrogen cyanide, acrolein, and ammonia, as well as carbon monoxide. These gases can be fatal in very small amounts.

- *Your instincts tell you not to.* If you are uncomfortable with the situation for any reason, let the fire department do its job.

The final rule when preparing to fight a fire is to position yourself with an exit or means of escape at your back before you attempt to use an extinguisher. In case the extinguisher malfunctions or something unexpected happens, you must be able to get out quickly. Don't allow yourself to become trapped.

Types of Extinguishers

The three most common types of fire extinguishers are as follows:

1. *Water or APW*. APW stands for "air-pressurized water." APWs are large, silver extinguishers that are filled about two-thirds of the way with ordinary tap water, then pressurized with air. In essence, an APW is just a giant squirt gun. APWs stand about 2 feet tall and weigh approximately 25 pounds when full. They are designed for Class A (wood, paper, cloth) fires only. Water does a poor job of extinguishing flammable-liquid fires, and if used on an electrical fire, there's a risk of shock or electrocution. APWs extinguish fire by taking away the "heat" element of the fire triangle. APWs are found in older buildings, particularly in public hallways. It is important to remember that electrical equipment must be disconnected from its electrical source before using a water extinguisher on it.

2. *Carbon dioxide extinguishers*, which are designed for Class B and C (flammable liquid and electrical) fires only. Carbon dioxide (CO_2) is a nonflammable gas that extinguishes fire by displacing oxygen or taking away the oxygen element of the fire triangle. The carbon dioxide is also very cold as it comes out of the extinguisher, so it cools the fuel as well. CO_2s may be ineffective at extinguishing Class A fires because they may not displace enough oxygen to put the fire out; Class A materials also may smolder and reignite. You can recognize a CO_2 extinguisher by its hard "horn" and lack of a pressure gauge. The pressure in the cylinder is so great that when you use one of these extinguishers, bits of dry ice will shoot out of the horn. CO_2 cylinders are red and range in size from 5 to 100 pounds or more. In the larger sizes, the hard horn is located on the end of a long flexible hose.

3. *Dry chemical extinguishers*, which come in a variety of types. You may see them labeled "DC" ("dry chem"), "ABC" (for Class A, B, and C fires), or "BC" (for Class B and C fires). It is extremely important to identify which types of dry-chemical extinguishers are located in your area. Read the labels and know their locations. Dry-chemical extinguishers put out fire by coating the fuel with a thin layer of dust, which separates the fuel from the oxygen in the air. The powder also works to interrupt the chemical reaction of fire, so these extinguishers are highly effective. Dry chemical, or "ABC," fire extinguishers are filled with a fine yellow powder. The greatest portion of this powder is composed of monoammonium phosphate. Nitrogen is used to pressurize the extinguishers. ABC extinguishers are red and range in size from 5 to 20 pounds.

Make a PASS

It's easy to remember how to use a fire extinguisher if you can remember the acronym PASS, which stands for Pull, Aim, Squeeze, and Sweep.

1. *Pull the pin*. This will allow you to discharge the extinguisher.

2. *Aim at the base of the fire*. If you aim at the flames (which is frequently the temptation), the extinguishing agent will fly right through and do no good. You want to hit the fuel.

3. *Squeeze the top handle or lever*. This releases the pressurized extinguishing agent in the extinguisher.

4. *Sweep from side to side until the fire is completely out*. Start using the extinguisher from a safe distance away, then move forward. Once the fire is out, keep an eye on the area in case the fuel reignites.

Testing and Maintenance

Give equipment a visual inspection each month and a maintenance check each year. Extinguishers with pressure gauges are easy to check. Extinguishers should be hydrostatically tested whenever they show new evidence of corrosion or mechanical damage. Fire-safety experts recommend that CO_2 and water models be tested every five years—every twelve years for dry chem and Haylon. In addition, dry-chem models should be emptied and refilled every six years.

The Fire Barrier

What You Need to Know About Fire Curtains, and Why They're Important

BILL SAPSIS

Theater fire curtains are seldom seen, rarely used, and are commonly misunderstood. Yet understanding what they do and how they work literally can be a matter of life and death.

A hundred years ago fire curtains were made of asbestos. The laws back then stated that you had to have the word *asbestos* written on the front of the curtain and that you had to bring it down and show it to the audience before every performance. While some of those laws still may be on the books today, most theaters do not show their fire curtain to the audience—and new curtains are not made of asbestos, which has been identified as a possible carcinogen. Since the mid-1970s, fire curtains have been made of other materials, usually a silica-based yarn or a fiberglass-based material.

There are two main reasons for having a fire curtain. The first is to seal off the involved (that is, burning) area from the noninvolved area. The curtain helps restrict the flow of oxygen to the fire, thereby helping to starve the flames. The other reason is to give ample time for the audience, cast, and crew to evacuate the building safely.

When a fire curtain is activated, it should lower in about 30 seconds and completely seal the proscenium opening. If there is a gap between the curtain and the proscenium opening, anywhere around the perimeter of the curtain, oxygen will be pulled quickly into the fire. If your theater has automatic smoke doors in the roof over the stage, the situation can become even more dangerous. The oxygen will flow faster, creating a chimney effect that causes the fire to burn very hot and very fast. When checking the curtain operation, ensure that it overlaps the top and side walls and touches the floor along the entire width of the opening.

Different Varieties

There are two basic types of fire curtains: the straight-lift curtain and the Braille curtain. A straight-lift curtain is hung like a backdrop. It's installed when you have enough height above the proscenium arch to lift the curtain out of sight when it's not in use. If your proscenium is 16 feet high and your stage roof is 40 feet, for example, you can lift the curtain straight up and have it disappear behind the proscenium. If there is a fire, the curtain can lower and cover the proscenium opening completely.

A Braille curtain is used when there is not enough height above the proscenium to raise the curtain out of sight: a 16-foot-high proscenium opening and a 28-foot-high stage roof, for example. With a Braille curtain, you would dead-hang the top of the curtain from the building steel and attach the lifting cables to the bottom.

Both types of curtains require rigging to function properly. The straight-lift style can be run by a counterweight system, an electrical winch, or a combination of the two. The Braille curtain uses a manually operated hydraulic winch. What all the rigging systems have in common is how they are activated/used/tripped.

How They Work

It's easy to see how a fire curtain is used (tripped) when you are in the theater at the time of a fire. You smell smoke, you see the fire, and you go over and pull on the fire curtain rope or push a button and the fire curtain comes down.

But what about when no one is there?

The first line of defense is the automatic fire release line, which is a rope or cable rigged along the proscenium opening. It is attached to the floor on one side of the opening, and runs up that side, over the stage, and down the other side. In a counterweight system, the line is then attached to the operating rope of the fire curtain.

In a Braille system, the line is attached to the brake handle of the hydraulic winch. Along the length of the line is a series of fusible links, which are designed to burn through and let go at approximately 160 degrees. There should be at least two links in each section of the release line and they must be part of the line. In other words, if a link separates, the fire release line also separates.

The fire release line is in tension at all times. When a fire starts on stage, the temperature rises very quickly. When it reaches 160 degrees, the fusible links separate, causing the fire release line to part, which activates the rigging system and lowers the fire curtain.

In many states an electronic release system is also required to be "in line" along with the fusible links. The electronic system usually has a sensor-activated electromagnetic switch. The switch holds the release line in tension; if the sensor is activated, the switch is released, releasing the fire release line, and the curtain is lowered. The sensors are usually either the smoke-detector type or the kind that measures the rate of heat increase.

One problem with a fire release line is that it tends to stretch over time. When it stretches, the fire curtain tends to creep down, eventually coming into view. When that happens, you have to go back to the release line and adjust it.

Another problem is that the fusible links aren't that strong. Over time the solder that holds them together may break, allowing the curtain to come down. To help solve this problem, the fusible links should be replaced every five years or so. A common mistake made to correct this problem is to chain the bottom of the counterweight arbor off to the building steel or otherwise tie the arbor up so it cannot move. This means the curtain will not work unless there is someone there to undo the tie-off; a fire in the middle of the night will go unchecked.

Maintenance and inspection are keys to keeping a fire curtain operational. The curtain should be tested and inspected at least once a year. And please remember that there is more to fire curtains than can be discussed here. If you have any questions about your fire curtain, contact the curtain manufacturer, the rigging installer, or your local fire marshal's office.

The money spent on maintenance and inspection is a pittance compared to the cost of a fire.

21 Headed for a Fall
It's the Most Common Accident, But It's Preventable

ELBIN CLEVELAND

C ommon falls are the most prevalent accident and the second highest cause of injury and death—behind only automobile accidents, according to the National Safety Council. In fact, falls cause 12,650 deaths per year, more than two million people sustain severe injuries, and millions more suffer from unreported accidental falls.

Falls are probably the most common accident in your theater and scene studio, too. So if you want to see an immediate reduction in injuries (as well as damaged equipment or products), begin by reducing the fall potential in your work environment. Here are sixteen simple (and mostly free) things you can do.

1. *Provide adequate lighting to illuminate changes in level.* While falls on a level surface are much more common, falls from one level to another are much more dangerous. So preventing falls between levels is the first place to take preventive action. It is much easier to avoid an obstacle if you can see it. The semi-darkness back stage and the deep darkness of a blackout are common causes of falls in the theater. Light those areas with generous amounts of glow tape, with LED indicator lights, or with shielded "lime lights."

2. *Provide bold warning signs and ribbon barriers.* Studies have proven that people can look directly at a sign and not really see it. Of course, some people always think signs do not apply to *them*, and thus ignore the warning. Therefore, the bolder the signs and ribbons, the better.

3. *Provide OSHA-standard physical barriers between different levels.* The standard rigid barrier should be 36 to 42 inches high and should withstand a lateral force of 100 pounds at any point along its length. A rope or a chain stretched across an opening does not meet this requirement.

4. *Insist that workers wear fall-arrest gear where appropriate.* If you don't have such safety gear and attachment points installed in your theater and studio, budget for them at once and install them as soon as possible. Insisting that they be used costs nothing.

5. *Provide adequate handrails at permanent changes of level, at stairs, and at ramps.* The tradition is always to place a stair handrail "on the right hand descending." However, a handrail on both sides is safer. Stairs 6 feet wide or more may require a center handrail as well.

6. *Keep the floor clean of sawdust.* Loose sawdust on a smooth floor is a serious danger. (You should have dust collectors on every tool anyway. See Chapter 27, "Bite the Dust.") If sawdust and chips are not collected automatically, insist that each worker take the 30 seconds necessary to sweep the sawdust into one out-of-the-way pile.

7. *Keep the floor clean of debris.* Place a waste receptacle by each stationary tool and insist that scraps and cut-offs are placed directly in the receptacle and not dropped on the floor. This also saves picking them up later.

8. *Keep the floor clean of liquids.* Wet floors are a major hazard. Mop up spills immediately or use absorbents and then sweep or scoop them up. Finally, use a floor fan to quickly dry the cleaned area.

9. *Remove or reduce small changes in floor level.* Nonlevel floors are a major trip hazard. Use flat thresholds wherever possible. Sand down uneven floorboards. Grind down uneven concrete and patch broken concrete. Fill cracks and holes with latex concrete.

10. *Make sure fatigue mats, carpets, runners, entrance mats, etc. lie perfectly flat.* Curled edges and large wrinkles are trip hazards.

11. *Install or paint slip-resistant coatings on all ramps and stairs.* If you can't afford a commercial product, mix clean washed sand with leftover scene paint and use that.

12. *Eliminate extension cords on the floor.* OSHA suggests overhead cord reels as a solution. If you can't do that, at least use brightly colored ones (orange or yellow), which are easier to see and thus to avoid. If you can't afford to buy new extension cords, buy a can of "safety orange" spray paint and paint your old ones.

13. *Eliminate all air and vacuum hoses on the floor.* Failing that, paint the ones you have orange.

14. *Encourage workers to use a workbench instead of the floor.* This gets materials and tools up off the floor, out of the way of others.

Work is usually easier on a workbench anyway. If you lack bench space, budget now to build more. If you lack floor space for that, use rolling workbenches or fold-up wall-mounted versions.

15. *Encourage and plan for the rolling of heavy props and scenery.* This strategy eliminates potential lifting injuries and, if a worker stumbles, there is nothing to drop or fall on a foot or ankle.

16. *Teach proper lifting and carrying techniques so workers follow safe practices.* Walking backward makes stumbling more likely. It also practically ensures that the dropped load will fall on the carrier due to its forward momentum and the worker's reduced ability to avoid it.

The Ladder of the Law

22

The Right Way to Scale the Heights

ELBIN CLEVELAND

Safety and reliability must be your first concern with ladders, not your last. It may sound simplistic, but because ladders are designed to climb upon, they are in a different category from other scene shop or theater accessories. So, let's start at the beginning, and work our way up. No matter what your theater's budget, this is one place where safety must outweigh economy. Think carefully about that before you make a purchase.

Choose the Right Type of Ladder

Don't buy a 14-foot stepladder when what you really need is an A-frame ladder. Don't buy an articulated ladder—hinged so it can be bent—just because the sign says it also will work as a scaffold. None of the articulated ladders we have tested over the years have a wide enough stance to be safe as a scaffold. They're not even very stable as ladders.

Choose the Right Size Ladder

Many people mentally add their height or their reach to the height of a ladder and then say, "I can reach 12 or 13 feet high with a 6-foot ladder." No you can't—unless you're standing on the top step, which is the most dangerous place to be. In fact, you should never stand above the third step from the top of any ladder. If you use a ladder properly, your reach is—at best—4 feet beyond the ladder and 2 feet to each side. Buying a short ladder is shortsighted, false economy.

Buy Only Top-Quality Ladders with a Heavy-Duty Service Rating

All new ladders are required to have a designated weight-duty rating posted on the stiles of the ladder. When comparing prices, be sure they represent ladders with the same rating. Don't even consider cheap lightweight ladders; they are a lawsuit waiting to happen. Theater ladders get used by everyone, so they are abused as a matter of course. You need a ladder that will withstand such treatment.

Train Your Workers Carefully

Write up and post ladder rules in the studio or shop so the workers know you're serious about safety. You might include these warnings, among others:

- Never use a stepladder that is not fully open and locked.
- Never stand on the top three steps of any ladder.
- Never carry tools or materials up or down the ladder; have things handed up to you or raised on a rope.
- Never leave tools on the top of a ladder.
- Never work on any ladder by yourself. (If an accident occurs, you may need immediate attention.)

Store Ladders Properly

Ladders are designed to be used standing up and that's the best way to store them. They take up less floor space that way, too. Be sure you have a safety chain at least 7 feet above the floor so the ladder can't fall over on anyone.

Never store a ladder outdoors. All have some steel hardware or fittings that rust in the weather. Wooden ladders are susceptible to rain and moisture, solar radiation, insects and fungi, many chemicals, and temperature extremes. Aluminum ladders corrode and become stiff and awkward to use. Some fiberglass ladders deteriorate under solar radiation; so do rubber feet, rubber bumpers, and some types of synthetic fiber ropes used on extension ladders. Don't sabotage your investment by letting it literally weather away.

It's OK to store ladders horizontally as long as they have sufficient support. Hanging a ladder sideways from two widely spaced supports places unnecessary lateral strain on the joints and will accelerate the loosening of them. Wooden ladders can even warp when stored this way. If you must store ladders by hanging, provide solid support every 6 feet.

Inspect Ladders Regularly

Even though you have trained workers to inspect a ladder each time they use one, you can't rely on that. You must include all ladders on your regular safety inspection of the theater and its equipment. Look for loose bolts or nuts, loose rungs or treads, worn extension ropes, and properly functioning fittings. Lubricate, repair, or replace as necessary.

Remove Faulty Ladders from Use at Once

Don't wait until the next day. Don't even wait until after lunch. You know how chance works. That time gap is precisely when some less observant or less cautious worker will take the ladder, take a chance, and take a fall. It only takes a minute to apply a standard red "Out of Order, Do Not Use" tag. (You have them right there in your desk, don't you?) As an extra precaution, consider locking the safety chain so the ladder can't be removed from storage.

Use the Right Type of Ladder for the Job

Aluminum ladders are electrical conductors. They should *never* be used to focus stage lights or for any other electrical work.

Purchase and use a "stand-off" for single-section or extension ladders. A stand-off is a U-shaped device that bolts to the ladder so the arms of the U rest against the structure. Consequently, the top of the ladder stands away a foot or so. A stand-off will bridge window openings, increase stability, and improve ergonomics. It is also economical and lightweight; all in all, a very worthwhile investment.

Be Sure Ladders Are Properly Positioned and Supported

The angle of a ladder to a horizontal floor should always be about 75 to 80 degrees. This is the common angle for all fully opened stepladders. If you can't visualize that angle, remember the distance from the bottom of the ladder to the wall should be about one-third the height of the ladder. If the ladder is too steep, there is not enough pressure against the wall, so it can tip and fall too easily. If the angle is too shallow, the ladder feet may slip on the floor and the ladder will slide out from under you.

Any ladder that raises a worker more than 6 feet should be stabilized at or near the top. A small length of chain or a stout rope with a snap hook is easy to attach to most ladders. If the ladder can't be temporarily secured at the top, it must be stabilized by a second person at the bottom.

When Good Ladders Go Bad | 23

You've bought the right kind of ladder, you use it correctly and safely, and you make sure it's taken care of. But despite all your vigilant care, even the best ladders—like all tools and equipment—become used, loose, and potentially dangerous. Many theaters don't have the financial resources to buy high-quality new ladders, so it is useful to know how to properly repair old ladders to improve their safety.

Knowing the Right Steps to Take

*L*et's take wooden ladders first. The most important structural parts of any ladder are the vertical sidepieces or stiles. Inspect these carefully for splits or cracks in the side or bottom; any that you find must be repaired at once. Here's how.

Gently open the split a little with a sharp knife. Use a thin wire to work carpenter's glue into as much of the split as possible. Then clamp the area, remove the excess glue with a damp shop rag, and wait 24 hours. Do not nail or screw the split! This can cause more splits and weaken the ladder irreparably. If the stile needs more reinforcement, add a metal hose clamp over the split and secure the clamp screw with a drop of Loc-Tite™. (Loc-Tite is a liquid thread-lock, commonly used to secure the bolts on machinery and bicycles and to prevent loosening from wear and vibration. A similar product is ThreadLocker™.)

Next, examine the steps or rungs. Be sure the steel rod under each step is tight. If not, tighten it, and secure the nut with a drop of Loc-Tite. Wooden rungs can come loose and rotate in the socket. If you find any of these, use a glue injector and a wood-swelling glue, which penetrates the wood fibers, causing them to swell and thereby tighten the wood joint. Then drill an undersized hole, and drive a four-penny finish nail (as they're called in hardware stores) through the stile and into the rung.

Wooden steps that are cracked should be glued and reinforced with a piece of 1/4-inch plywood glued and stapled to the bottom side. Sand all edges of the plywood before you apply it. Broken steps should be replaced; use the old one as a pattern. Be sure to use good wood for the replacement. You can cut anti-slip grooves in the top surface with your router.

Wooden stepladders and extension ladders have metal fittings that can become worn and loose. Sometimes the hole where the bolt or shaft passes through the wood has become enlarged. If so, remove the old bolt, redrill the hardware, and install a bolt of the next larger diameter. Use self-locking nuts or a drop of Loc-Tite to prevent loosening.

Finally, make sure the ladder is stable laterally. Even good ladders can rack (become out of square) and wobble back and forth. This unexpected shift can cause workers to lose their balance and fall. To correct this problem lay the ladder face down on the workbench and measure its diagonals (from opposite corners). Clamp one stile to the workbench and move the other one until the diagonal measurements are equal. Then clamp the second stile.

Next, cut one or two 1/4-inch plywood gussets (triangular braces) to fit your ladder. Sand all edges; then seal with one coat of shellac or varnish. Apply the gusset(s) to the back of the lower steps and the stiles with narrow-crown pneumatic staples. Do not use nails or screws! If you do not own a pneumatic stapler, use 1-inch wire nails. They are very thin and will not split the wood. If the rear edges of the steps and the stiles do not align, you may have to add a small filler piece. (Do not add gussets to the top steps of stepladders, as this may prevent them from folding closed.)

The rear legs of stepladders also can have racking problems. Correct this with gussets or by adding wooden diagonal braces. Follow the same procedure to confirm that the frame is straight before you brace it.

Similar repairs can correct the same problems with aluminum ladders. Most aluminum ladders are assembled with machine-installed aluminum rivets, which become loose with time. If you have a heli-arc or an inert gas welder, you can straighten the ladder and then weld all the riveted joints. Do not over-weld. Welding a frame can cause metal stress from the heat expansion and contraction; use small "tack welds" instead. If necessary, you also can add aluminum gussets or diagonals. Small aluminum plates and flat bars are available at all large hardware stores.

Damaged fiberglass ladders are the most difficult to repair. Often the only safe option is removal from service and disposal. Sometimes a cracked stile or tread can be reinforced by bolting in a length of wood or a metal angle. If gussets or diagonals are required, they should be bolted in place with small-diameter bolts. Use toothed lock washers under the bolt head and the nut to spread the stress on the fiberglass.

When your ladder collection is repaired as well as possible, consider making some improvements to further increase safety. For example, the rungs or steps of older wooden ladders may have become smooth with use. Make them slip-proof by adding self-adhesive, anti-slip strips purchased from the hardware store; by painting the tops with an anti-slip pumice paint, from the same source; or by adding no-slip rubber treads. For the latter, old auto floormats work well—they can be cut into strips and glued or stapled in place.

You also might add a permanent pulley and hand line to long ladders so workers don't have to carry items up and down. And paint the top three steps red and label them "NO STEP" as a warning. Since no one should stand on the top step anyway, add a permanent tool tray so tools are less likely to fall and break or strike workers below. (Metal bread pans work well.) If you have an outdoor theater or use your ladders outdoors, add pivoting "shoes" to the ladders to provide a bigger "footprint" and prevent sinking into soft ground. Include the rear legs of stepladders.

If your workers have to use 110-volt tools while on the ladder, eliminate dangling power cords by permanently running one up the back of the ladder with a multiple receptacle at the top and a male plug a few inches from the bottom. That way you can run two power tools or one tool and a work light and there's no chance the worker will trip over the cord on the way up or down.

Some multipurpose stage floors are polished and slick. Reduce the chance of ladders slipping by gluing or stapling a piece of rubber to the bottom. Pieces of inner tube, auto floormat, garden hose, or doormat all work well.

Frequently, the best safety improvement is one that discourages misuse. If you can't keep workers from climbing to the top of the ladder to work, simply remove the second and third rungs or steps. This will not reduce the working strength of the ladder, but will stop senseless acts of bravado. If you can't prevent workers from using the bucket shelf on a stepladder as a step, remove the shelf. You don't need it if you have a permanent tool tray on the top step.

If you fear that workers will use ladders unwisely while you are elsewhere, lock the safety chain holding them to the wall. If you are concerned people may use extension or A-frame ladders to reach closed areas or dangerous spaces, chain the extension so the ladder won't reach.

These simple steps can eliminate most of the physical hazards of ladder use. The personnel hazards will always be there. Repeated training, insistence on following the rules, and setting a good example are your best weapons.

A Leg to Stand On

24

The Supporting Role of Beams and Platforms

ELBIN CLEVELAND

S turdy, well-built beams and platforms are essential scenic components, and since platforms are normally supported by legs, which raise them above the stage floor, determining their strength is also critical.

Wood can fail for two reasons: from compression of the cells and from bending. A leg can support the maximum load under compression when it is fully vertical and prevented from moving out of plumb or bending. This maximum load varies with wood type, but both common construction woods—Douglas fir and Southern yellow pine—have a compressive strength of around 1,200 pounds per square inch. All calculations are based on this maximum load.

It may seem simplistic, but engineers classify legs as short, medium, and long. In a short leg, the least dimension of its cross section is equal to one-tenth or less of its total length. In other words, a 2×4 leg that is 15 inches or less is considered a short leg. (Measurements reflect the size before the lumber is trimmed for shipment, so a 2×4 actually measures $1\frac{1}{2}$×$3\frac{1}{2}$ inches.) Since a short leg is in no danger of failure from bending, it will support its maximum load—that is, its compressive strength per square inch—without any need for bracing, *assuming* that the load is bearing straight down and no lateral loads are at work.

So, to determine the strength of the leg, you must know the ratio of length to width.

A medium leg has a ratio of least dimension to length between 11 and 24. Medium legs can be long enough that there is some danger of failure from bending under the maximum load. These legs will support between 99 and 67 percent of the maximum load without diagonal bracing, based on the same assumption used for short legs.

Long legs with a ratio higher than 24 are prone to failure from bending well before the maximum compressive load is reached. Such legs never should be used on stage without additional bracing to stiffen them. You can use diagonal bracing or add reinforcement to the least dimension of the leg, making it thicker.

Diagonal bracing reduces the long leg to an intermediate size, based on the space between the diagonal braces. To maintain the maximum strength of an intermediate leg, the bracing must be repeated every 36 inches ($1\frac{1}{2}\times24$). The diagonal bracing should be placed *perpendicular* to the $3\frac{1}{2}$-inch face of the 2×4 since $1\frac{1}{2}$ inch is the least dimension.

In general, the maximum load on a leg is determined by the compressive strength of the material and the cross section of that material. The maximum load on a 2×4 leg of Douglas fir or Southern yellow pine is equal to 1,200 pounds per square inch times $1\frac{1}{2}$ inches times $3\frac{1}{2}$ inches—or 6,300 pounds, more than 3 tons! Even the longest intermediate leg with a 67-percent capacity will support more than 2 tons.

So what's the problem?

The problem is that other, often-overlooked factors are at work that can quickly cause the actual strength of a 2×4 leg to weaken dramatically. If instead of Douglas fir or Southern yellow pine you use a 2×4 of fast-growth softwood like spruce or white pine, the legs will have barely more than half the strength of Douglas fir. If a medium leg is 67 percent of a short leg (many platform legs are more than 15 inches tall), and if that leg is spruce, then the maximum load under ideal conditions drops to 2,517 pounds.

Second, calculations are based on properly seasoned, new lumber. Nearly all theaters reuse lumber that has been screwed, nailed, drilled, and bolted. Used lumber will further reduce the strength. A $\frac{3}{8}$-inch bolt hole through the center of the $1\frac{1}{2}$-inch dimension reduces the volume of wood at that point nearly 25 percent. The maximum capacity under ideal conditions immediately drops to 1,887 pounds. If this $\frac{3}{8}$-inch hole is not drilled along the center line, stress on the leg increases because the load will be unevenly distributed on the wood that remains, and the maximum capacity will be even less. And more bolt holes will further reduce the capacity.

Third, calculations are based on a lumber grade of "construction or better," which is more expensive than the lower grades found in outlets where many budget-conscious theaters buy their lumber. These lower grades have larger knots and splits and are less straight-grained and often less well seasoned. Such defects can reduce the basic strength by frightening percentages. White spruce wet from exposure or incompletely dried has only 49 percent of the strength of a 2×4 with a standard moisture content—this reduces the capacity to a mere 924 pounds! It is possible to purchase 2×4s from chain stores that you can actually break over your knee.

At this point, you may say, "So what? Even at 50 percent of strength, a short leg will still support 3,150 pounds. I don't have any actors who weigh that much." Let's hope not. But there are still other factors to consider.

Remember that the short leg with straight downward force is the ideal situation, rarely the real one. Every time a standing performer takes a step, he or she "pushes off," creating lateral force on the platform and the legs up to 40 percent of the actor's weight. Even diagonal bracing may not help much in such cases.

Just stepping up on the platform can produce a downward force 1½ times the actor's weight. Stepping down from a platform only 6 inches above produces a still higher load. Running, jumping, and dancing can produce a downward shock up to 2½ times the actor's weight. That shock must be combined with whatever lateral force is exerted when the actor lands and stops the forward momentum. None of this will be well received by low-grade, used lumber filled with bolt holes.

If the maximum strength of this medium leg is 941 pounds, its real strength will be somewhat less. To compensate for this difference, engineers always incorporate a safety factor into their calculations—that is, they build the structure as if it were going to support a higher load than anticipated. The *minimum* safety factor for self-standing structures is 2:1. That means the maximum load on this medium leg should not exceed 924 divided by 2. That's 462 pounds, which is a very low load indeed—when you consider that one 200-pound actor stepping down from a higher level will exceed this limit.

What's a poor technical director to do?

Begin with new, good-quality lumber, free of large knots and other defects. Examine used lumber carefully before you use it in critical applications. Use only Douglas fir or Southern yellow pine on structural units. If you must use white pine or spruce, downgrade the capacities by 40 percent. Strengthen any 2×4 leg more than 15 inches long with diagonal bracing to the platform or to the floor. Finally, remember that the leg and the platform are only as strong as the joint that connects them. The configuration of that joint and the hardware used on it all figure into the strength of the finished structure.

25 | *Flying Scenery Safely*

If there are so many backstage dangers on the ground, what about the problems when something needs to go up in the air? Yes, the risks increase significantly, which is why careful attention must be paid.

How to Rig Your Flats Correctly

Anytime you hoist something in the air, it has the potential to fall and injure someone. That is why the minimum safety factor for rigging—5:1—is almost twice the standard construction safety factor of 2:1 or 3:1. That is, a system that is expected to hoist 1 pound should be able to handle 5 pounds without a problem. (A factor of 8:1 for rigging is common and 10:1 is not unusual. At a 10:1 ratio, a 100-pound load would require a flying system with a safe capacity of 1,000 pounds!)

Note that "system" here means that *all* elements of the support must have a capacity at least five times the static load imposed on them, not just the support lines. It is foolish and dangerous to fly scenery with a 2,000-pound-capacity steel cable and then make the attachment with an unrated S-hook from a local hardware store.

Draperies are the most commonly flown scenic element. Usually they are not considered dangerous because they are soft goods. They also have tie lines all along the top that distribute the weight of the curtain and are fastened directly to the pipe batten. This is also true of most manufactured backdrops, the second most commonly flown scenic element. While the draperies are soft, the pipe is not, and certainly presents a hazard if it should fall.

However, the real problems begin when you start to fly rigid scenery such as flats. The reason is that common construction methods used for flats are designed to hold the flat together while it is resting on the floor, not while it is suspended overhead. Traditional soft (fabric-covered) and hard (plywood-covered) flats are assembled using compression joints, not tension joints. The weight of the unit against the floor provides the compression, and the familiar 1/4-inch plywood corner blocks and keystones mounted with staples are only strong enough to keep rails, stiles, and toggles in place.

However, 1/4-inch plywood is *not* strong enough to carry the tension load of the entire flat suspended in the air, where the cable is pulling in one direction and gravity in the other. The taller and larger the flat, the more weight the top corner blocks must support and the greater likelihood they may fail. So the first rule for flying flatwork scenery is never to suspend it by hanging it from above. It always should be supported from below, as if it were standing on the floor. The best way to do this is first to run support lines from above all the way to the bottom of the flat, where they are properly joined to a hook hanger iron.

Second, always use appropriate flying hardware that has been designed for that purpose and purchased from a reputable theatrical supply house. Never use a piece of hardware from a local hardware store that has an unknown load capacity. Just because it looks strong enough doesn't mean it is.

Third, be sure any hardware used is attached properly. Flying hardware should never be attached with nails because they easily can pull out under stress. The same is true of wood screws, even though many pieces of hardware have countersunk holes that suggest they can be mounted that way. Unfortunately, wood screws also can be pulled out easily under stress. This is especially true under a shock load, which can occur any time the batten hangs up or fouls momentarily. The sudden release from the hang-up will create a downward force many times the normal or static load. A screw barely 3/4 inch long has very little holding power in soft woods (such as pine and spruce) commonly used for flat construction. It will not withstand the shock load of a scenic unit that free falls for even a few inches.

The only safe way to mount hardware is with bolts that pass all the way through the wooden frame and the hardware piece. An attachment secured with bolts will fail only if the wood itself fails. Either flathead stove bolts or carriage bolts will provide a secure attachment with little disruption of the scenic surface.

The support lines may be natural or synthetic fiber rope or steel cable as long as they provide the minimum safety margin of 5:1. Remember that any type of fiber rope weakens as soon as it is tied in a knot in order to fasten it to the scenery. In fact, most common rope knots reduce the rope strength from 30 to 45 percent; knots that sharply kink the rope may reduce its strength by more than 50 percent.

Fiber rope also weakens when it passes through a small-diameter eye or ring that forces the rope to bend sharply. Steel cable is a much safer choice. It is stronger for its size and you can purchase appropriate hardware for properly fastening it to the flatwork.

Although there are many types of steel cable, only two are commonly used in the theater. Standard wire rope is made of plow-grade steel and uses larger wires than aircraft cable, and so is less flexible. It may be used for heavy items such as the lighting bridge or the orchestra shell. Aircraft cable is the common choice for theater rigging because it is thinner and more flexible, making it less visible to the audience and more adaptable to smaller sheaves and fastenings. Most aircraft cable is galvanized, which means it will resist rust.

Wire rope is like fiber rope: it should never be kinked. A kinked wire rope already has a reduced load capacity and should be discarded, or the kinked part cut off. Wire-rope attachments always should be made with an approved wire-rope clamp (also called a cable clamp). If the cable passes around an object less than an eighth of the cable diameter, a wire-rope thimble (a specially curved piece of metal) should be used to prevent sharp bends in the cable. In other words, a $1/8$-inch aircraft cable should not be passed around a diameter less than 1 inch without a thimble for support. Not doing so places highly unequal stress on the inner and outer wires and can lead to catastrophic failure.

Wire rope clamps have two halves: a yoke and a saddle. The saddle should always cover the load (or live) side of the wire rope before it passes through the thimble. The yoke always should cover the tail (or dead) end of the wire rope.

Be sure to check this position carefully, for it is critical to the security of the fastening. Locate one cable clamp next to the thimble and a second clamp 3 to 6 inches away. Tape the end of the cable with ordinary electrical tape so it won't fray or unravel. When the clamps have been placed, use a socket wrench and tighten the nuts onto the yoke alternately. Be sure the yoke remains straight in the saddle and the two cable lines are straight in the clamp. As the nuts become tighter, be sure both are tightened to the same degree.

When the wire rope is firmly attached to the bottom of the flat(s), go to the top of the flat and pull out any slack. Bolt a second hanger iron or a cable guide to the top of the flat. Be sure this piece of hardware is aligned with the one below. As always, tighten all bolts the same amount so stress is equalized.

If you bolt hardware to the bottom of the flat and if you use wire rope, thimbles, and clamps carefully, you should never have to worry about scenery falling from above.

How to Handle Runaways

26

Perhaps you didn't quite follow all the instructions about how to fly scenery safely. You may run the risk then of a serious problem. Here's advice in case that occurs.

What to Do When Things Go Flying

*I*t's one of the most dreaded backstage mishaps. Someone involved in loading or unloading a batten's counterweight (such as a sandbag or a metal block or "pig") loses concentration. The batten, and whatever is attached to it, becomes unbalanced and comes crashing down or—just as dangerous—goes flying upward with great force. In technical theater parlance, this is a *runaway*.

If a batten starts to creep, you may be able to stop it by brute strength alone. However, once the batten and its contents start to move quickly—meaning it is seriously out of balance—do not attempt to stop it. As much as you may want to save whatever is attached to the batten, to do so could cause serious injury.

Instead, if a runaway occurs, shout a warning to all crew members, then take cover. Everyone should protect themselves from flying counterweights or other hardware. Depending on the situation, the batten will either go up or down, and it's more than possible that it will hit adjacent flown objects, accompanied by snapping lift lines, falling loft blocks, and activated sprinkler systems. The only reasonable course of action is to act quickly and get out of harm's way.

As with all safety issues, the best way to deal with runaways is to avoid them. Train crew members to concentrate on the task at hand. Sometimes people become so used to handling rigging that they forget just how much weight and potential force they are dealing with.

The correct way is to first lower the batten to the floor. If the batten and its contents are heavy, make sure you can hold it all down until the counterweight has been loaded. Second, load the counterweight. Third, raise the batten slowly a short distance to test for balance. Fourth, add or subtract weight as needed for final balancing. To unload, return the batten to the stage floor. Carefully unload the counterweight, then remove whatever is attached to the batten.

Bite the Dust

Working with Wood in Your Scene Shop Can Be Dangerous

ELBIN CLEVELAND

27

The International Agency for Cancer Research has demonstrated unequivocally that airborne dust is a potent carcinogen nearly as serious as cotton and coal dust over the long term. Unfortunately, the results of this review of more than 350 case studies have not made their way into the theatrical knowledge base.

One study that examined the health and work history of eighty-two men who had adeno carcinomas showed that eighty had chronic exposure to wood dust. An English study of ninety-eight men with nasal cancer found that 67 percent were cabinetmakers or chairmakers. A Danish study of 488 cases showed the risk factor for woodworkers was 30.

The normal risk factor for noncarcinogenic material would be 1.0, or no increase in cancer due to exposure to this material. We usually become concerned when the risk factor rises above 2.0, which means an exposed person is twice as likely to develop cancer as one who is not exposed. The general risk factor of lung cancer for smokers compared to nonsmokers can be as high as 15. So, the risk factor for wood dust is *twice* that of tobacco—yet we frequently do virtually nothing to protect ourselves, coworkers, or students from airborne wood dust.

The most dangerous dust is from "oily" aromatic woods such as walnut, cedar, redwood, and mahogany. The chemicals in these woods, which give them moisture or insect resistance, are especially damaging to the lungs. If you have cut any Luaun mahogany plywood, you probably not only smelled the difference, but also actually felt it in your throat and lungs as you breathed.

Manufactured wood products that are bound together with various resins are another major hazard. As we continue to destroy old-growth forests and move more and more to manufactured lumber made from chips, fibers, strands, and dust, this problem will only increase. Anyone who has cut Masonite knows how insidious that fine dust is. What you may not realize is that the dust is filled with the chemicals used to prepare the sawdust or wood chips to bind it into sheets.

Many industrial companies and wood industries have been aware of this for years and already have dust-collection and air-cleaning systems in place. Theaters must do the same—and it's not hard to do so. For instance, almost every hand tool is now available with a vacuum fan and dust-collection bag. In most cases the bag can be removed and a vacuum hose connected in its place. Even ten-year-old tools may have such a system and can be purchased as reconditioned from tool-supply companies at prices well below the cost of new tools.

If you can't replace your old tools with new(er) ones, there are several other options that will protect people in the scene studio. Most are very inexpensive.

■ Make sure all workers wear paper-fiber dust masks when sanding or creating fine wood dust. While this is more critical for the worker using the sander, these tiny airborne particles affect everyone.

■ Create a flow-through ventilation system for your workshop. (You need one anyway to replace stale air contaminated with the mixture of fumes generated in a typical scene studio.) If you don't have the money, stack a pair of window fans in a wheel-away rack and place them in front of a door or window. (Be sure to add a dust shield for the motors and remember to clean the fan blades regularly to maintain efficiency.) If this airflow creates a significant loss of heat or cooling, you will have to purchase a commercial exhaust system with an integral heat exchanger.

■ Devise an attachment for your shop vac and get a long and flexible vacuum hose that can be joined to the specific tool being used. If you don't have a shop vac or have several tools operating at once, go to a used-appliance store or a flea market and buy one or more used canister vacuums exclusively for this use. They can be permanently mounted under the workbench with a remote-control switch mounted on the side.

■ Be selective about the tools you modify first. The worst offenders are those that produce the fine dust particles that float in the air. (Chips and pieces that won't float in the air won't get into your lungs.) Sanders and high-speed miter saws are the worst offenders, while drill presses and joiners may not require any modification.

■ If you have a window or an exterior wall, build your own exhaust hood. Any fan will work as an exhaust force, but since there may be heavy concentrations of dust here, look for a fan specifically designed for exhaust. Or use a TEFC (totally enclosed, fan-cooled) motor. Wood dust and air are an explosive mixture—the sparks from exposed motor brushes could cause an explosion.

■ Buy or build your own dust-collection table on which all sanding can be done. Cover a table frame with a top of open-work materials, such as lathing, hardware cloth, or grillwork. Perforated hard board is a simple choice. Build a dust-proof enclosure underneath the frame and attach it to the dust-collection system or shop vac.

■ You also can invest $1,500 to $2,000 and a day's time in the installation of a permanent full-shop dust-collection system. A larger work area may require two collectors and more piping, which can double the cost. If so, plan ahead so two separate systems can be installed efficiently. Be sure to include a crossover connection so you can use either collector if one isn't working. Most home centers and hardware stores have the parts you'll need and a handbook to help design the system.

One important caution: In your attempt to keep dust away from workers, do not use portable fans to create an air flow past the workers. Air currents from fans loft the fine dust particles farther into the air, where they linger and pollute a larger volume of space for longer. If you must use fans to combat summer heat, mount them on floor stands or on the wall and aim them above workers' heads where they will still circulate the air while raising less dust. Never use floor fans in a scene shop.

Whatever solution you choose, don't delay. Take some action now and plan to incorporate further changeover costs into next year's budget. This is important for the health of your workers, and it's a good strategy to avoid health-based lawsuits in the future.

28 Getting Everybody Out Safely

Sometimes, you can't stay around and fix the safety problem, whatever it is. You must leave the theater premises, and do so immediately. And there is a correct way to do that.

In an Emergency, Everyone Must Know What to Do

ELBIN CLEVELAND

While audience safety may be thought of as a front-of-the-house issue, the truth is that emergency doors often open into backstage areas. During a fire, tornado, or earthquake, people are just as likely to rush to the stage doors as to the lobby. Thus, all backstage personnel should know how to help evacuate the theater safely.

Audience safety is a greater concern at intermissions and after the show, when hundreds of people want to go to the same place at the same time. The problem is magnified because many audience members are talking to each other about the show and may not always watch where they are walking. And, of course, people who are hurried or frustrated often make bad judgments that can lead to accidents.

Therefore, one of the best safety measures is to improve traffic flow and to make sure your audience has sufficient time during intermission. Have clear signage for directions. Use ushers to give directions and assistance.

A typical intermission problem is refreshment and concession stands, which often are understaffed and too close together. If your lobby space permits, consider the use of several refreshment islands located far apart. Staff them with enough people to serve everyone during the first two-thirds of the intermission. That will give patrons time to finish their refreshments without hurrying. Then workers can spend the last third collecting cups or glasses while the audience returns to its seats at a casual pace. Be sure a sufficient number of waste containers is present and located near, but not obstructing, the audience route. These containers should be removed before the final curtain when the audience makes an exodus *en masse.*

Also remember that although the emergency exit paths may never be used, most state laws require they be checked within an hour before the house is opened for every performance. Some organizations require that a staff member inspect every exit path all the way to the street and report to the house manager before the house is opened. Any blockage that requires correction should be noted in the house manager's daily report so it can be prevented before the next performance.

This is the same thing the stage manager does for the backstage areas. Although backstage emergency exits may not be intended for public use, the law requires they be treated the same. They are not spaces to store half-empty paint buckets, fake muskets for Act II, or semiretired directors.

Exit halls and stairs must be well marked and well lit. They cannot contain folding chairs, coat racks, or technician's bicycles. Anything loose can be knocked down and fallen over. Such passages also must be free of any combustible matter such as costumes, extra stage draperies, unused decorations, stored paper products, and old programs.

In many cases, the exit path leads down a fireproof stairwell or corridor. All doors that open into these passages must be equipped with "panic bars" with latches and automatic door closers. The closers and latches prevent air pressure of a fire from blowing doors open and filling what should be a secure area with smoke and toxic fumes. Never allow workers to prop those doors open with stage weights or to tape down the latches.

You don't have to have a catastrophe to have a serious injury and consequent legal problems. A single patron who chooses to use the emergency exit for any reason must have a clear passage to the street. One stumble over a backstage dustmop that shouldn't have been there will make you or your company liable for medical bills and a host of other expenses, possibly including fines for obstructing the passageway. Even a member of the company could use this infraction to recover medical expenses. Post signs that inform all workers that these exit passages must remain clear; mark the path with industrial marking tape. Be sure the passages have emergency lights in case of a power failure and test them to make sure they work.

Remember that all doors through the proscenium wall are

supposed to be fireproof. They should have automatic closers and latches like those on emergency stairways. Again, do not allow workers to prop open these doors with stage weights or other objects, or to tape down the latches. Doorways through the proscenium that have only a drapery covering are strictly illegal; they won't block fire or smoke and are easily pulled down, becoming a trip hazard when many people try to make a hasty exit.

Don't stop inspecting at the exterior exit door. Look outside as well. Exterior emergency exits should have a clear 8-foot space beyond the door opening. Do not allow unused scenery, trash cans, dumpsters, or parked cars to infringe on this space.

If the exit path includes a fire escape, follow it all the way to the ground. If the lowest section of the escape descends mechanically, check to confirm that it is not chained off, that it operates smoothly, and descends fully to the ground. Do not permit obstacles to impede its descent. Again, mark off the "clear area" below the escape with signs, paint, and industrial marking tape.

The last thing to do is to check all public areas before the lights are turned off and the doors are locked. Although it is rare, there have been cases where people have fallen asleep or taken ill and then were locked in the building. (Thieves sometimes hide as well; always have two people check the facility.) When you are confident that everyone has left the building, you can sigh, lock up, and go home.

Since You Asked

29

Zip Cord, Real Food, and Duct Tape

Q. I have heard from two reliable sources that zip cord [also known as lamp cord] is illegal for theatrical purposes. Is this true?

A. Zip cord is not necessarily illegal, but it may not meet local code requirements, depending on the use. Most table lamps, chandeliers, stereos, and other small household devices are wired with zip cord, so it has its proper uses. It should not be used where the code calls for "hard use" (i.e., permanently wired) rated cable, or where a grounded plug is required.

Since zip cord is only two-conductor (that is, not grounded), it is not Underwriters Laboratory (UL) approved. If your municipality requires only UL-approved wiring devices be used in public venues, then do not use it. However, some temporary installations are usually allowed. Lamps on end tables in the lobby, for example, usually past muster if they have a UL sticker, even if they use zip cord. (It's difficult to find table lamps that *don't* use zip cord except in hospital supply stores.) Zip cord is usually allowed to feed audio to intercom headsets, or to connect a temporary loudspeaker to an amplifier. But zip cord is not an option for permanent AC installations. Most local requirements follow the National Electrical Safety Code, which sets forth what is appropriate for permanent installations, for fixture wiring, and many other details.

Most NES codes are referenced in the OSHA regulations. In cases where OSHA regulations prevail, zip cord violates the grounding requirements in 29 CFR 1910.304. "The minute you have even one employee in a privately owned or nonprofit theater, OSHA rules apply," notes Monona Rossol, of the New York-based Arts, Crafts and Theater Safety Organization. "If the theater is run by a state, county, or municipal government, then the rules may or may not be the same, depending on where they are located."

Q. For an upcoming production, we are going to be cooking real food over real fire, since the play takes place in a restaurant.

79

The director wants the look of a real kitchen, so that means a gas stove. Any advice?

A. You'd better check with your local fire department to see if it requires you to have an open-flame permit, a propane permit, or a special-effects permit. You probably won't be permitted to operate the stove on stage unless you can prove to the fire marshal that you know what you are doing and that your setup is safe. (In that case you may be required to hire a licensed special-effects person to handle this for you.)

If you do get permission, the simplest and safest way to make your range is to strip a camping stove and mount it into a counter top, pumping it (the fuel must be pressurized first) before the play opens. Have an appropriate fire extinguisher handy. The safest approach, however, is to use a properly installed electric stove.

Q. To keep people from tripping over the sound cables back stage, I plan to cover them over in traffic areas with duct tape. It's a two-week run and then I have to strike. Will duct tape leave a residue on sound cable and extension cords and, if so, what can I use to remove it?

A. Taping down cables is an excellent safety precaution. There are a number of solvents that will remove residue from your cables. The citrus-based type is less toxic and more environment-friendly. Both Citra-Solv™ and Goo-Gone™ work well, as does plain rubbing alcohol.

You can avoid getting residue on the cable in the first place. Many tape manufacturers make "tunnel-tape," which has no adhesive down the center (lengthwise), so there is little or no residue. More time-consuming, but cheaper and just as effective, is wrapping toilet tissue around the cable before you tape it down.

Tape is not the best solution, however, because it leaves small ridges where shoes can catch. You can place rubber mats over the cables, with the edges taped to the floor with gaffer's tape. The mats can be used over and over again, and a 3×5-foot mat can be cut in half to 3×2.5 feet, which is a better fit for most requirements. (Carpet scraps turned upside down may also work, but be sure to tape the edges down carefully.)

Perhaps the simplest solution—although expensive—is cable cover. Sold through computer supply stores and catalogues, this flexible product is 3 inches wide and comes on a 25-foot roll so you can cut it to the desired length. It's higher in the center, with a indentation on the bottom running its entire length, into which the cable fits. A roll sells for about $45—about $1.80 a foot.

Did You Know? | 30

Where There's Smoke

Millions of installed smoke detectors don't work because of dead batteries, damaged electrical components, blocked vents, or parts failures. Test your detectors monthly. Some units have a built-in check by which you shine a flashlight into a sensor to see if the unit works. Others have a test button. However, neither method really replicates the conditions of a fire (the test button simply tells you whether there is power in the detector), and some units have no checking system at all. A test recommended by many fire departments is the use of a smoke simulator. One such is the appropriately named Smoke Detector Tester™. You spray the aerosol can toward the smoke detector for a second to two; if the detector is working, an alarm will sound, which usually stops in less than a minute. To stop it sooner, fan a newspaper at the detector. The cost is $5 to $10 per can, depending on the size can. To locate a local distributor, contact Home Safeguard Industries in Malibu, California, at 310-457-5813 [e-mail to distrib@homesafegard.com].

Triple Threat

Combining safety, convenience, and security in one package, motion-sensitive floodlights make a sound but inexpensive investment for many theaters. Once installed, they will turn on as a truck pulls up to the loading dock or a worker approaches the back entrance to your theater. They also help deter prowlers. Motion-sensitive lights are available at lighting and hardware stores for as little as $30.

Have a Plan

Do you have a clearly defined emergency plan for accidents and medical emergencies? It's a wise idea to write one and post it where it can be seen back stage. You should have a clear system of handling emergencies worked out among stage-management personnel as well. The system should designate who keeps the show running, who calls for an ambulance, and who helps the person with whatever first aid is required. Make sure you have an easily accessible backstage first-aid kit and that you check frequently to keep it stocked. A good basic supply includes bandages for minor cuts, ammonia inhalant (smelling salts), hydrogen peroxide (antibacterial), ice packs, and a small oxygen tank and mask. Such supplies also may be used for accidents or injuries involving patrons; large theaters may want to duplicate the kit for use by house management staff.

Pass the Word

Create a fire code word or phrase. That way, if there is a fire you can signal others without alarming the audience. If the stage crew can handle the situation, there may be no need to concern your patrons. If the fire does require evacuating the theater, you will gain a few precious moments to organize your staff to handle the situation and avoid panic.

The Person in Charge

The stage manager is the obvious point person for the safety of any production, says long-time stage manager Peter Lawrence.

"As stage manager you are the *only* person who knows not only what the actor is required to do—because you've been in the rehearsal hall—but also what the set is required to do and when, and what the problems are for that set," he points out.

That's important, he says, because "something might appear completely harmless, like a flight of stairs. But *you* know that what the actor has to do as he or she is running down that flight of stairs is inherently dangerous. And you have an obligation to speak up."

Lighting the Way

Many theaters have hallways that lead from the dressing rooms or green room to the stage. During performance, the hall lights are turned off, often making the journey a hazardous one for actors in a hurry between costume changes. A simple way to light the path is the use of photoelectric night-lights. These plug into any wall outlet and turn on automatically when the other lights are turned off. These lights also are useful in other places where ambient lighting is likely to dim during performance.

Get It Right

Double-check your backstage area to make sure you have a fire extinguisher that is safe for electrical fires. One theater company found its extinguisher was water-based only after a cable shorted out. Luckily, the fire was put out before someone used the extinguisher; it was only when the fire department investigated that the lack of a dry extinguisher was noted and one was installed.

THEFT

S afety is not only an important question for your staff and volunteers; your property and premises need to be safe, too. They need to be safe from the thieves and vandals who can strike anywhere, of course, including a theater. A well-run back stage is the first defense against this kind of damage. In this section you'll find practical tips on safeguarding tools, equipment, storage, entryways, and personnel.

31 | Don't Give Thieves a Chance

How to Protect Your Theater Against Loss

Stephen Peithman

Theft and vandalism is a crime of opportunity. If you make it easy for someone to steal, police say, chances are good someone will. The situation in the theater is no different, whether through burglary or petty theft involving workers or visitors. Unless your bank account is unlimited, preventing theft is vital to your company's long-range health. And while thieves may have an eye on front-office hardware, it's backstage doors and windows that are the prime entry point for burglars and vandals.

The Basics

Fortunately, putting the brakes on breaking and entering is relatively straightforward. Crime-prevention experts say thieves aim for the door or window that is most vulnerable to forced entry. By making unauthorized entry difficult, time-consuming, and noisy, you can discourage most break-ins. And when you add specific security measures to the mix, you've gone a long way toward defending yourself against theft.

Here's a summary of the ways you can make your theater building more secure.

Lights. ■ Proper outside lighting eliminates shadows, which burglars need for cover while they attempt to break in. All points of entry should be lighted, including those on the roof. When you leave the theater at night, leave some lights on inside just as you would do at home.

Locks. ■ Make sure doors, windows, skylights, and other openings are secured with the best possible locks. No lock is burglar-proof, but the longer and harder a burglar finds it to break in, the more likely he'll simply give up.

Windows. ■ Check window frames to see if they're loose or rotting. Also make sure the windows are not blocked. From inside you should be able to see any potential danger that lurks outside—just as people passing by your facility should be able to see any suspicious activity inside. Check to see that the view is not blocked by boxes or set pieces on the inside or high shrubs outside. If windows have been painted over, consider removing the coating. In some cases window bars may be called for; if so, make sure they have spring mechanisms that release from the inside in case of fire.

Doors. ■ Replace all hollow-core doors with solid-core models; hollow doors are easy to punch or cut a hole through, allowing an intruder to reach the lock inside. Exterior doors with glass or thin panels are particularly vulnerable. You may want to consider replacing glass in or near the door with security glass or plastic, or affixing a shatter-resistant plastic film to the inside surface of the glass.

Fences. ■ If you have fences around your property, they should be high and sturdy enough so they aren't easy to leap over. This helps keep out vandals as well as burglars. Again, in case of fire, these should have a safety release so no one is trapped trying to escape.

Alarms. ■ Although it may often feel like it, people really aren't at your theater 24 hours a day, seven days a week. If break-ins during down times are a major concern, install an alarm to deter burglars or force them to leave quickly if they break in. Be sure to post warnings in clear view that your business is equipped with an alarm, and train your staff how to avoid setting off false alarms.

Safes. ■ If you have a safe or cash drawer on the premises, minimize the amount of cash on hand after hours. If you keep cash or other valuables in a safe, make sure it is anchored to the floor, in an illuminated location visible from the outside. Change the combination from time to time, police advise.

If these steps seem overwhelming, consult with your local police department. It's likely an officer will inspect your facility for problem areas and advise you on any of these prevention measures.

Other Steps

Law-enforcement officials and insurance investigators recommend the following procedures to safeguard your facility.

■ Restrict keys to staff who actually need them. Keep up-to-date records on who has all copies. If an exterior door key is lost or stolen, change the locks immediately.

■ Label keys by color or code rather than by what they're used for. (Would you want a burglar to find a key marked "power tools"?) Lock up all office sets of keys.

■ Ask for identification from all repair people who come to do work at your facility.

■ Store valuables out of sight from the outside; there's no sense tempting someone who happens to pass by.

■ Keep an inventory, recording the make, model, serial number, distinguishing characteristics, and purchase price of all equipment, and place identifying marks on your valuable property. (Take advantage of free or low-cost registration programs run by many police stations.) Display stickers in prominent locations to tell thieves you've marked your property.

■ Appoint at least two staff members to check the premises before closing and run through your security checklist. Inspect all closets, bathrooms, and other places where a thief might hide while waiting for you to leave. A cordless phone is an ideal companion—if you believe there is an intruder, do not confront him; call the police immediately.

■ Before closing up each night, double-check all windows and doors to make sure they are securely locked. The best hardware is useless if you have an "open-door" policy. (It happens more often than you might think.)

■ If you have a burglar alarm, make sure it is set before the last person leaves.

■ If, despite your precautions, you are burglarized, call the police immediately. Don't enter the building or office if you see signs of forced entry. Leave the crime scene just as you find it, and don't open the doors to employees or volunteers until the police give their OK.

Internal Theft

It's bad enough when an intruder breaks into your theater, but when staff, volunteers, or visitors steal, you're left dealing with both the loss and the betrayal of trust. Here are some precautions you can take, depending on the size of your operation.

Begin by reminding staff and volunteers not to make theft easy, whether it's the company's property or their own. The first rehearsal or tech meeting in the theater is a good time to mention these basic guidelines:

- Don't leave out money or valuables.
- Don't bring expensive jewelry or electronic devices to the theater.
- Mark your personal items, using an engraver.
- Don't leave your property unattended.

For larger theater companies, the following measures may be useful:

- Separate purchasing, receiving, and accounting roles to reduce the autonomy in any one job. When two or more people are involved in a particular function, they police each other.
- Control purchase orders by prenumbering them (in sequence), and get supporting documentation for each purchase of expense invoice.
- Close the register or cash drawer after every transaction. All transactions should have a receipt.
- Never leave office keys hanging on a nail or in the lock, where they can be borrowed and duplicated.

Make it company policy that theft of any kind will not be tolerated. Some managers overlook losses sustained through internal theft or go easier on the perpetrator than they would on a stranger. It is better to send a clear signal that discourages theft and helps everyone in the theater feel they are in a safe place.

32 | Alarm Systems for Theaters

Interior Versus Perimeter Protection

Most often, the best way to minimize theft and vandalism is to take simple, obvious, common-sense steps. When burglars hit the Huntington Playhouse, a nonprofit community theater in Bay Village, Ohio, the theater lost a computerized sound board and a Minidisc player from the tech booth. According to the theater's technical director, Tom Barnett, a patio door that was secured by a deadbolt was forced open. The booth itself was not locked.

The theater's insurance was not expected to cover the equipment's replacement value. "The moral of the story," Barnett says, "is lock up your equipment." He also thinks a good security system would have helped in this case.

But what kind of alarm system should you have?

The best alarm systems for many theater buildings are designed for perimeter protection—to prevent the intruder from entering the premises. Systems that rely on interior protection alone present two potential problems. First, they allow the criminal to enter the facility before the alarm is sounded. (When there are staff or volunteers present, the danger is obvious.) Second, due to the nature of the component parts of these systems, they cannot be used without limiting normal activity within the facility. Most important, however, is the simple fact that perimeter protection emphasizes personal safety, while interior protection primarily protects property.

From a practical standpoint, however, probably the greatest degree of protection is afforded by a system that combines perimeter protection with one or more interior sensors that can be turned on or off independently of the perimeter devices. Since no system is foolproof, this procedure provides backup protection in the event an intruder succeeds in violating the perimeter. In addition, it makes practical the design of a "limited" perimeter system—one that protects the most vulnerable accesses, but not every means of entry through the perimeter. Care should be exercised in such situations to use devices that avoid accidental activation and that blend with the use of your theater.

Hardware

At its most basic, perimeter protection refers to sensors installed on doors and windows. They set off the alarm whenever a window or door is forced open. Full perimeter protection means every possible point of entry has a sensor. Interior protection, on the other hand, refers to a motion sensor being used to detect someone inside. Putting full perimeter protection on a theater is expensive, but this is the best way to ensure that the alarm will go off before the intruder gets inside.

Installation of the perimeter devices is straightforward, while the installation of interior sensors can be tricky. (If you have a theater cat, a "pet alley" will be necessary to avoid false alarms.) The installer must be careful to avoid putting the sensors where heating ducts or the sun's rays can cause temperature changes that might set off a false alarm. Price of the sensors also determines accuracy. More expensive sensors often have higher immunity to false alarms. They also have formulas and double-checks that reduce the effect of temperature changes, insects, and flapping drapes creating false alarms. Dual technology sensors, using both infrared and microwave detection, reduce false alarms and cost more as well. Two sensors also may be aimed at the same area from different angles and wired to require dual activation before sending in an alarm. Again, this reduces false alarms and doubles the price.

Two or three perimeter detectors backed up by a motion sensor is the most inexpensive possible layout; it also is easy to violate. Since most false alarms come from the sensor, and presumably a cheap layout will use a less expensive sensor, it may tend to cause more false alarms. Reasonable perimeter protection (cover on the most accessible windows and all doors) with good motion sensors, well placed, gives adequate protection. Audible sirens may be considered to scare away intruders. A good system should have a remote keypad at a convenient location for entries/exits. The "brain" or "guts" to any system is the control panel, which should be in a remote location.

A number of companies make glass-break detectors, devices that set off an alarm when breaking glass is heard. They tend to be sensitive to similar sounds, like jingling car keys or a dropped plate in the prop area. If adjusted to avoid false alarms from anything other than the actual window panes, they may not work when those panes are actually broken. Fortunately, burglars rarely enter through broken glass. They reach through a broken pane to unlock and open the window frame or door. (Burglars don't want to get cut either). Opening the frame or door then sets off the alarm. Therefore, glass-break detectors should be used only when a massive glass area represents the obvious entry point and careful calibration must be used for effective detection.

Hard-Wired Versus Wireless

Hard-wired systems run wires through your walls and floors to connect the sensors. The advantage of a hard-wired system is dependability. There are no batteries to change. The sensors are easily concealed. The disadvantages to hard-wired systems are that they take longer to install and require drilling walls and ceilings, as well as lifting carpets, during installation. Wireless systems' sensors transmit a radio signal when they detect an intrusion; no wires are needed. They can be installed in a few hours with less mess. Changing the system later is easier. Wireless systems do have batteries that must be changed; most should be replaced annually. More expensive lithium batteries last three to five years.

Supervised Versus Unsupervised

Supervised systems tell you when a door or window is open. They indicate if a sensor is not working, usually meaning a battery died. With most, the alarm control panel also tells where the problem is. When you leave open a door or window, or if a sensor is not working, you won't know it with an unsupervised system. Your alarm will be set but a window may be open.

Off-Premises Monitoring

A proper burglar-alarm system should feature a distinct signal on the premises, both inside and outside. In this manner, the occupants, the intruder, and the neighbors are alerted at the same time. The alarm signal may be a loud bell, buzzer, siren, horn, or other warning device and also may be installed with various automatic lighting features that either turn on the household electric lights or activate special emergency signal lights. Warning decals or similar emblems affixed to the theater's points of entry are also useful in deterring intruders.

The mere fact that an alarm system exists is often sufficient deterrent to discourage a burglar even before he tries to force an entry. In addition, the local alarm signal is generally enough to scare off most intruders once it sounds.

Silent alarms that do not sound on the premises but merely alert an off-premises monitoring source are not recommended for some locations, since they allow the intruder inside, into a position to threaten an occupant while police respond to the silent signal. However, the procedure of transmitting an alarm signal off the premises to a monitoring location is an excellent additional form of protection when used in conjunction with a local alarm. Such an off-premises alert means help will be on its way quickly in an emergency.

Alarm signals are generally transmitted via direct connection to a central monitoring station by means of special leased telephone lines or by various forms of automatic telephone dialers utilizing the existing household telephone line. In the latter approach, there is a dialing device that utilizes a digital dialer to transmit a special coded signal. Where combination alarms are installed, the transmitter should differentiate between the various types of alarm signals— that is, fire, burglary, or medical emergency. Systems should be capable of pinpointing the location of an intrusion within your theater; such a feature is certainly an advantage to the police officer responding to an alarm signal or to a technician trying to locate a problem sensor. The central station employs trained personnel whose only function is to remain alert for alarm signals and to act upon them, which usually involves immediately dispatching either alarm company personnel, a private guard service, local police, or fire officers to the scene.

Two-Way Voice Monitoring

Two-way voice monitoring may be considered to help reduce false alarms and provide help in case of a fire or medical emergency. Here, an amplified intercom is installed in your facility. During an emergency the intercom is turned on and the monitoring center speaks out through it, challenging the intruder. The dispatcher can be heard throughout the facility. (Larger theaters require remote speakers.) If the signal is a medical emergency, the dispatcher immediately asks if a medic is required. The dispatcher can stay on the line until the ambulance arrives and give instructions to the medics. They arrive knowing the situation, who the victim is, the physical condition, and how to get in. If the signal is a fire, the dispatcher can verify it without anybody needing to come to the phone. If the signal is an intrusion, the dispatcher will verbally challenge.

Audible or Local Alarms

Care should be exercised when choosing an audible alarm or an externally audible component to a monitored system. Alarm systems that sound externally should include a "reset" feature to prevent the continuous sounding of the alarm. Many cities have noise-abatement laws prohibiting noise that disturbs the peace, comfort, and repose of others at any time. If your theater is located near a residential area, this can be a problem. What is the likelihood of the alarms being heard? What will the response be from the people who would hear the alarms? Will the alarm be ignored, acted upon, or treated as a nuisance?

Selecting the Right Alarm Company

While it is possible to obtain alarm components for "do-it-yourself" installation, such systems can provide a false sense of security. They normally do not provide full coverage of the theater, may not be of the same quality as a dealer-installed system, and can be false-alarm–prone unless installed by a person of sufficient technical skill. Select a well-established company with a record of successful operation behind it. The failure rate among companies entering the field is high and you don't want to be left with a system that requires service with no one to do the job. Business and trade associations are excellent places to check on a company before you invite anyone into your theater. This way, you can eliminate in advance the likelihood of being pressured by an unsavory or disreputable company. Make sure any employees who have access to your facility are bonded. Here are some additional points to consider:

■ Does the alarm company have errors and omissions insurance? Are there any hidden costs?

■ Does the alarm company meet industry-accepted standards? Underwriter's Laboratories certification is a quality-assurance program that will ensure your alarm and monitoring company are following standards in installation, equipment use, and business practices.

■ Does the alarm company program have an adequate training program in the use and operation of its alarm system?

■ Does the alarm monitoring company have access to a bonded and insured keyholder service?

■ Is alternative first-response service available?

A security system designed for your specific needs using today's technology and proper installation gives you peace of mind for years to come and provides trouble-free operation.

Power Backup and Other Quality Issues

An alarm system is only as good as the reliability of its power supply. The most dependability is provided by a system that operates on regular electric power, with emergency backup power provided by a battery to assure operation during emergencies. A rechargeable means of automatically reporting battery failure should be included. In addition, a service and maintenance contract that includes automatic battery replacement when needed is highly desirable. Here are some other quality checks:

■ Some visual or audible signal should be provided to alert you to a malfunction in the system prior to operation.

■ Any components that can turn the system on or off, or render it otherwise inoperative or ineffective, should be tamper-resistant.

■ A quality system should carry a reasonable warranty covering both parts and labor, from both the manufacturer and the installer, for a period of one year from the date of installation.

■ The alarm system should be capable of being easily upgraded at minimal cost to meet changing needs—smoke, fire, medical, water, temperature, or legal requirements.

■ Since any system of this type will require service from time to time, you must be sure the company you deal with can provide it promptly.

■ Make sure you understand your system thoroughly. Be aware of what it does and does not do. You should be made familiar with all the details of operating the system, and receive verbal as well as written instructions covering all circumstances.

■ The alarm system also should be easy to learn to operate for everyone who may require access to your premises. Equally important, you should cooperate with local crime-prevention programs, as well as all reasonable requests and requirements made of alarm-system owners by your local police.

By properly registering your system and advising authorities of whom to contact if you are away when your alarm sounds, you will greatly assist them in providing maximum protection to you, your staff, volunteers, and audience.

SETS AND LIGHTS | PART VI

*T*he sets and lights that illuminate your production are the visible face your audience sees, the onstage results of your hard work. But running lights and set shifts during technical rehearsals and actual production is a major focus of backstage activity. It takes planning, coordination, and hard work to make sure all the hard work isn't visible—particularly when the circumstances change. Sometimes, it takes specific tools to make sure the lighting equipment or the scenic pieces don't provide a danger themselves. Those who work back stage must learn to live with all that equipment, to repair it when necessary, and to be prepared for the possibility of last-minute adjustments.

Now more than ever, the effort back stage must be a collaborative one, even as each person assumes distinct responsibilities and accepts them completely.

33 | *Shifting into High Gear*
How to Organize Efficient Set Changes

Set changes must take place quickly, silently, and safely.

We know one technical director who, during rehearsal, discovered that one set change was taking 15 minutes. Clearly, this would never do. She asked the crew to come in before the next rehearsal, and with some careful replanning, the change was cut to 10 minutes. She went home, and the next night came in with a new plan that reduced the shift time to under 3 minutes.

How did she work this miracle? The same way a director helps actors improve line readings and movement. She blocked the shift and she had the crew rehearse it. Each time they got better, and each time the crew itself came up with ways to make things go even more efficiently. Here are some ideas to help you do the same.

Break It Down

Probably the most time-wasting element in any shift is people waiting for others to finish some task. So break the shift down into its smallest components. The smaller the assignments and the more people you have, the faster the shift will go.

For example, if a wall unit is composed of three flats hinged together, you may need three to six people to handle it. They may have to wait until furniture and props are removed, but if the wall is in pieces, one or two people may be able to begin separating them before the furniture is removed. As soon as the obstacles are safely out of the way, the walls can be removed quickly.

So, take a look at the set, determine how many individual pieces there are, in what order they need to be removed, and where they are to be stored off stage. Then assign people to take care of each element. Finally, rehearse the sequence until everyone feels comfortable with it. (Be sure to write it down, so that replacement crew members can catch up on what's expected.)

In some cases, you may need someone to do something as basic as pull back a drape until a set piece is rolled off safely. (If you're short-handed, actors not in the next scene can be asked to help.) Lawrence Stern's book, *Stage Management* (Allyn and Bacon), gives excellent examples of charts you can use to plan and supervise your scene shifts.

A Place for Everything

Make sure that all ladders, tools, and other equipment needed for the shift are located in one place just off stage. If you don't have space off stage to store all these items, have crew members bring them near the end of the scene or act. You may need to rehearse this as well since there may be noise problems, and they also may be in the way of actors and other stagehands.

Some Specifics

Speeding up set changes may take more than rehearsal—you may need to devise changes in the physical setup as well. Mounting units on wagons is one way to move heavy objects with greater efficiency—often by only one or two people. However, since a wagon is basically a platform on casters, it easily can go astray. If you use rigid casters and attach strips of wood to the floor to create tracks, you may have less difficulty. The strips should be nailed or screwed to the floor, and must be out of the way of actors.

Almost everyone uses wagons for scenery shifting at one time or another; unfortunately, some do not use wagons big enough. If the set on the wagon has a wall, it must be supported from the back so it does not shimmy when the wagon is moved. Lining up the wall with the back of the wagon provides the maximum amount of useable floor space, but it doesn't provide support to the wall. The answer is simple: either accept less floor space or use a larger wagon. In addition, you can fit the wagon with four cross braces, each with a pair of casters. This not only adds strength, but also prevents the wagon from creaking and groaning. Remember, if your audience notices that sets shimmy and creak when moved, you have already lost the illusion you have worked so hard to create.

Another solution is the revolving platform: a circular unit on casters, fastened to a pivot at the center, and revolved by hand. These can be expensive to build, however, and if not well-constructed, are again liable to squeak and groan as they are turned. Some special design problems arise as well—the back of one set is now the front of another, and somehow the two must work together.

The simplest solution for the stage manager is the visible shift, in which lights are dimmed and the crew (and cast, in some cases) moves the set in full view of the audience. If the director is ingenious, this even can be worked into the show. Audiences love to see the workings of a production, and it is often better to use the visible shift than to have them wait in the dark in front of a closed curtain. If a set crew is used to shift in full view of the audience, they should wear dark clothing (long-sleeved black sweatshirts and pants are ideal) of a neutral style that does not clash with the period of the play.

We saw a production of *The Importance of Being Earnest* in which the crew was dressed as house servants. While two men moved a couch, a "maid" gave a table a once-over with a feather duster, then removed books and a pillow. A "butler" flirted with a "cook" who came on to remove a luncheon tray. Several workmen in period clothes did the hard labor. A stage manager can help a director spot such opportunities early in the production planning.

The One Essential

It cannot be stressed too often that a successful set change is the result of thorough planning. The technical director needs to specify the sequence for shifting the set. This is important, because the integrity of the pieces may be compromised if they are not handled appropriately. Post the set shift instructions prominently on both sides of the stage. That way, if anyone has a question about the sequence of events, they do not need to find the stage manager or technical director for an explanation.

Planning also means that every person involved understands their role—and that of the others—in the shift. It's foolish for any one person to see only their part in the process. Everyone involved needs to know what leads up to their task, and what follows their timely completion of it. If a crew member knows that he must remove a chair before a wall can be moved on, he's more likely to move quickly. Also, if one crew member is ill or injured, another may be able to fill in because she understands the entire process.

Have Set, Will Travel

34

As difficult as set changes may be at your theater, imagine the increased level of difficulty when you need to move your production from one venue to another—and then move again. While the problems of touring a production may seem unique, they do in fact illuminate a number of solutions for set questions at any theater.

On Tour, Keep It Light, Keep It Flexible, the Experts Say

Nancianne Pfister

Taking a show on the road, whether to a festival or as part of a tour, presents its own logistical problems. One of these is having the proper set for your performance, designed with travel in mind.

In the ideal world, your company has enough money to call the local professional moving company and pay them to dismantle and transport your massive set. In the less-than-ideal world, you may have to move it yourself. That move begins with the design.

Gayle Bowling, general manager of Theatre West Virginia, lists her company's standards for a set design that will travel hundreds of miles to schools in the outlying areas. "Keep it simple and interesting," Bowling explains. "Our marionette set is standard each year. For our children's show, the set needs to be easy to load and unload. It must fit whatever vehicle is available to transport it."

Since the configuration of stage spaces will vary, it is important that the set be instantly adaptable. "We take a black curtain and a set of colored boxes," Bowling says. "The cast members wear black jumpsuits and the boxes hold props and costume pieces." The curtain can be used as a backdrop or to define spaces on stage.

Weight and versatility are always a factor. Diane Crews of DreamWrights, a children's theater in York, Pennsylvania, says a portable set must be "lightweight, but sturdy. It has to be colorful because we work with kids. It has to be foldable. It has to fit the truck, car, or van you will be using to move it."

This last may be the most overlooked requirement, according to Crews. "I found out the hard way how important it is to measure everything. Not just the set pieces, but the vehicle you'll be using. You have to measure it *inside*, with the doors or tailgate closed. If you don't always have the same vehicles at your disposal, build your set to suit the smallest one available."

Boxes seem to be a staple of the moveable show. Crews uses them to replace all other furniture. "You can stand on them, sit on them, stack them, or hide behind them," says Crews. "The big ones are tables; the small ones are chairs. They get hard use, so they must be sturdy." To make them easy to manipulate on stage, boxes must have handles. Stick-out handles take up space; it's cheaper to cut holes in the tops and sides of each box instead. To further save space, build the boxes to nest.

Maximum flexibility is important, which is the reason Crews relies on folding screens, both as backdrops and for creating backstage space. "We use panels that are 5-feet, 9-inches high by 2-feet wide," she explains. "By connecting them with two-way hinges, we double their versatility. The frames are made from Luaun, which is very sturdy, but too heavy for the whole screen. We make the panels out of foamcore [available at craft stores and office-supply stores]. It's just two pieces of poster board with a thin sheet of foam between them. When we need to change a set, we just slide out the foamcore panel and put in a new one."

If your set will get minimal use, or if you want to create it on the spot as part of your presentation, cardboard is a lightweight and inexpensive choice. The Paper Bag Players of New York City have earned fame for their innovative props and costumes made of paper or cardboard. Delighting the younger crowd for years, they not only perform but also teach children how to make paper masks and other elements of stage fantasy.

The Bags production manager, Guy Gessell, votes in favor of the artistic set over the practical, urging designers to make things as big as they want. "The first thing the design team should *not* have to consider is that we will always travel," Gessell says. "They need to have freedom to create, not to think about smaller sets or lighter sets. I will figure out how to pack it. Paper is not hard to fold and to box."

The Bags carry their creativity in three fiberboard boxes 45×70×11 inches. The boxes protect the fragile contents and enable them to be shipped. Gesell urges more designers to explore the uses of cardboard. "We depend less and less on wood, even for frames," he says. "We want the look of boxes found-in-the street, loose and free-form. Cardboard is amazingly sturdy, but painting it the right way is important. If you use water-base paint it may chip after it dries and you'll have to keep repairing it. You need to use latex acrylic, which is costly, but saves money and time in the long run because it won't flake. Cardboard sets will last a long time—some of our sets are in museums."

If the set involved is complex or on a grand scale, such as might be needed for outdoor theater, Theatre West Virginia sends along a technical member of the company, one who not only works with the set but also with lighting and sound needs.

When you are preparing a show for competition or festival, you have the added requirement of a limited time on the stage. The American Association of Community Theatre's AACT/Fest allows only ten minutes before your performance in which to erect a set. The stage must be cleared within ten minutes after the performance.

Often represented at AACT competitions is Florida's Theatre Winter Haven. "We sometimes purchase a set and adapt it for our own before passing it on," says company director Norman Small. "But the competitive element changes the rules. We design a festival entry specifically to be set up and dismantled in a limited time."

If your set was not designed for portability, you may choose to take only key elements when you travel. The Footlighters of Burlington County, New Jersey, were invited to bring its production, *The Problem*, to AACT/Fest. The set had a complete living room, cumbersome and expensive to ship. Publicity director Ruth Iversen remembers, "We felt like carpetbaggers. All we brought was the bookshelf. The carpet and two chairs were already there." It may not sound like much, but it was enough to establish the scene.

Diane Crews likes an onstage three-dimensional look, so she designs sets in pieces, referring to them as a "puzzle." You might need a shrub or a tree, she says. "Make two pieces exactly alike and paint them. Then make a slot from the bottom center to the midpoint of one shrub piece. This is Slot A. Then cut a matching slot from the top center to the midpoint of the second piece as Slot B. When you want to use them, slide Slot A into Slot B and *voila!* You have free-standing shrubbery. This looks wonderful and it travels flat."

Just as you must pack your suitcase with appropriate items for your vacation, so must you plan carefully before taking your show on the road. Everyone we spoke with agreed that you cannot count on finding exactly what you need already in place at the site of your performance. Not even at Lincoln Center.

Softening the Hard Edges

35

Lighting Tricks to Protect Actors, Your Crew, and Your Set Design

KATHLEEN GRIFFIN

During tech rehearsal, performers bruise themselves running into wood-framed "legs" as they exit the stage. Packing your truck for a tour, you find you don't have room for the flats you use to frame the stage. Your lighting designer insists on clean edges but all you have are soft velour "blacks." Such problems are not uncommon. The question is, how *can* you achieve the look of hard-edged legs through the effective use of soft goods?

At I. Weiss & Sons, we have perfected a method that will work with almost any size piece and with most theatrical fabrics. And since it requires very little in the way of additional materials or construction, it fits the budget of most theater companies. You can modify existing fabric legs or create new ones out of velour or other theatrical fabric.

Whatever the material or the size, the basic concept is identical: thread bungee, or shock, cord through the vertical hem on the leading edge of the drape. The cord, stretched vertically from a hanging pipe above to the floor below, provides the hard edge, yet will flex when hit and spring back into place.

Using small, sharp scissors or a seam-ripper, open the top and bottom of the side seam on the leading (onstage) edge of the drape or fabric. The bungee cord will be threaded through this seam, so to make the job easier, first attach the cord to a small dowel or wire hanger. Work it down the hem and out the opposite opening, leaving extra cord sticking out at both ends.

You will need a length of cord equal to the height of the drape plus enough to tie it off at both top and bottom. To prevent the ends from retracting into the hem, knot the cord where it comes out of each opening. For the best look, the lower opening should not be at the bottom edge of the hem, but about 6 to 8 inches above. The extra cord at the top is then attached to the same pipe or batten that the drape normally hangs from.

Assuming you want the bottom of the leg to be level with the stage floor, have the bungee cord exit the vertical hem about 6 to 8 inches from the bottom. This allows you to adjust the tension of the cord without pulling on the bottom edge of the drape. If for any reason you end up with excess fabric on the floor, simply turn it under, away from the stage side of the drape.

How you attach the cord to the floor depends on whether you are free to screw into the stage itself. The fastest way is to install an eyebolt into the floor, through which you thread the bungee and tie it off. Or you can tie the cord to a dog clip (also known as a bolt snap) that you attach to the eyebolt. Another method is to screw an eyebolt through a small batten or piece of wood attached to the bottom of the drape, through the fabric, and into the deck. While this will create a hole in the fabric, it will also create a sharp, horizontal edge to the piece. Or you can use the eyebolt and batten as mentioned, but rather than attaching it to the fabric or screwing it into the deck, simply weight the batten with a sandbag or steel weight. This last method will also allow the tensioned piece to fly easily. Simply detach the bungee from the eyebolt; the cord stays in the hem as the piece flies, and a stagehand carries the weight and batten off stage.

Whichever method you use, paint the floor attachment a bright color (or use fluorescent paint) so performers don't trip over it. For a crisp look, attach horizontal battens to the back of the drape, fitted into duck-canvas pockets, which provide stiffness yet are easily removed for traveling or storage. Since most often you are only concerned with the look of the leading edge, the battens need not be wider than a width of fabric, typically 4 1/2 feet. Stiffening battens work best when spaced every 4 to 5 feet horizontally. Clean-edged, easily packed, and performer-friendly, these "hard" legs are an excellent choice for touring companies or wherever they can most effectively replace truly hard edges.

The Lighting Emergency Kit

36

It's almost a given when working with lights: something will go wrong, something will break down. And yet, despite the inevitability, frequently backstage crews aren't fully prepared to cope with these problems and breakdowns. That doesn't have to be the case.

What You Need to Assemble Your Very Own

MIKE BROMBERG

When you need a tool to fix a lighting problem, do you have to improvise or borrow it from the set-construction crew? There's a better way: put together a useful toolbox for your lighting department, to carry to productions or leave in the booth or back stage. Here's how.

Start with a big toolbox from the hardware store—the brightly colored molded plastic kind with a comfortable handle, a removable tray, and a reliable latch or two. If it has a few covered compartments for small items, so much the better. Stencil "LIGHTING" on the outside. Then get a combination lock to prevent the latch from falling open by itself; even if you paint the combination right on the toolbox, the lock will cut down on tool borrowing. (Consider putting a splash of distinctive spray paint on each tool to encourage its return.)

Wrenches

The most important tool for lighting is the adjustable or crescent wrench; keep a few on hand to pass out at hanging and strike time. The 8-inch size is most useful, although 6 inches is adequate. Tie a 4-foot length of cord through the hole in the handle that can be tied off to a belt loop to protect against dropping. Adjustable wrenches will need to be adjusted often, but unlike an open-end wrench will fit any bolt head you come across.

There are quicker alternatives to the adjustable wrench if your equipment is all fairly new. Altman makes a cross-shaped wrench that fits all its instruments (including the handwheels), but doesn't have a hole to which you can attach a cord (you have to use one of the wrench openings, which gets in the way). The Mega-Combo™ (from The Light Source) is a compact and lightweight tool, useful for focus and adjustment, but may not have enough leverage for hanging and strike (and it's missing a couple of important wrench sizes found on older instruments and clamps).

Ratchet handles and socket wrenches, popular in automotive work, are little used in lighting because of the need to change sockets and the difficulty of tying off. However, I have successfully used a Gator-Grip™ universal socket (from Endeavor Tools in Guilford, Connecticut), which contains spring-loaded pins and fits all the various sizes of square and hex bolts on lighting instruments.

Other Hand Tools

You will need screwdrivers, large and small, both regular and Phillips. I prefer a four-way screwdriver, which contains four snap-in tips. A tiny-bladed screwdriver (or a set of jeweler's screwdrivers) is also invaluable, particularly for connectors. Screwdrivers are the tools most often borrowed and least often returned; keep a few cheap, standard screwdrivers in your kit to lend out.

Some other useful hand tools to have: diagonal wire cutters, slip-joint pliers or channel locks, long-nose pliers, and a pocket knife (a Leatherman-style tool combines these two), locking pliers such as Vise–Grips™, scissors for cutting gel, tape measure, 6-foot steel ruler, Allen key set for tightening knobs and latching doors open, and an X-Acto™ knife and blades. Also, a magnifying glass, a flashlight (I prefer a HubbelLite™ micro-headlamp that clips to a baseball cap; it's made by Hubbel Lighting of Torrence, California), work gloves for handling hot instruments, pipe wrenches for assembling booms, cordless drill and bits, screw extractors and a tap wrench for removing broken bolts, and jeweler's files for leaning lamp pins and sockets.

Electrical Tools

These tools are what make this a *lighting* toolbox. Get an inexpensive volt-ohm meter and leads. Radio Shack has a good selection, both analog and digital—either kind will do. You will need ranges for measuring resistance (an audible continuity beeper is particularly helpful), plus DC voltages around 10 volts and AC voltages up to 240.

Although the meter can make all the measurements you need, some time-saving alternatives may be helpful. An AC-outlet tester plugs into any Edison outlet and checks for proper wiring in an instant. The GAM-Chek™ tool [from Great American Market] combines that outlet-tester function with a cable tester and lamp tester, and is handy if you use stage pin connectors. These have neon bulbs, which may glow even on an "off" dimmer due to leakage current.

You can make a useful test light by attaching a 7.5-watt incandescent bulb in a rubber construction-site socket to a male connector; the bulb acts as a minimum load on the dimmer, to avoid false readings.

You will need a crimping tool for fastening crimp lugs to wire. The best kind has a tooth in the crimping area (sometimes marked "ignition terminals") to put a dent in the lug; its jaws meet like this—)) rather than like this—().

Circuit-finder kits are available that let you trace audibly which circuit breaker feeds which outlet—useful if you often find yourself in unfamiliar theater spaces. An inexpensive light meter (Davis Instruments SLM-100) can help you detect and correct dark spots on stage. I use an inexpensive wattmeter (Davis Instruments DVW-1) to check lamp wattages without opening the instrument; it also can give an early indication of a lamp near the end of its life (lamp wattage measures more than 10 percent above or below the marked wattage).

Other useful electrical tools include a soldering iron, smaller and more versatile than a soldering gun; an Edison 3-pin to 2-pin adapter ("gozinta"); Edison grounding cube tap ("three-fer"); and alligator-clip test leads.

Marking Supplies

- white grease pencil for marking gels
- indelible markers (several colors)
- white indelible marker or correction pen for writing on black gaffer tape
- drawing template for marking changes on the plot
- pencils and pens
- eraser

- tags with string (red, yellow, green) for marking instruments
- gel sample books

Lubricants and Cleaners

- spray solvent oil (like WD-40™) for use only on clamp bolts
- powdered graphite for use on all hot parts of instruments
- contact-cleaner spray ("tuner tonic") for cleaning electrical contacts
- emery cloth or fine sandpaper for removing corrosion from electrical contacts
- rubbing alcohol in a small squeeze bottle for cleaning fingerprints off lamps
- facial tissues for cleaning lamps and lenses

Tapes

- vinyl electrical tape, black and colors
- friction tape, useful for making strain reliefs because of its thickness
- gaffer's tape: black, white, and colors (for fastening and marking; doesn't leave a residue like duct or masking tape)
- gel repair tape (doesn't become brittle under heat like Scotch Magic™ tape); available from some theatrical supply houses
- high-temperature woven fiberglass tape (not fiberglass packing tape; for repairs inside instruments); made by 3M and others, available at some electrical-supply shops or through an electronics distributor.
- tunnel tape, black and yellow striped, for taping cables down to the floor; available from theatrical supply houses

Other Supplies

- tie line (black cord)
- black foil; made by Rosco, Great American Market, Lee
- solder, rosin core, fine and coarse
- solder wick for solder removal

- crimp lugs, various sizes and styles (ring, spade, splice, butt)
- wire nuts, various sizes
- hookup wire—a few lengths of #18 gauge stranded Teflon-insulated, tinned-copper wire of various colors, useful for replacing broken or burned wires; available from Radio Shack or electrical-supply houses
- assorted screws, bolts, nuts, washers
- 9-volt batteries
- brass paper fasteners (¾-inch) for gel frames

37 | Since You Asked

Special Casters, Stabilizing Sets, Mixing Paint

Q. Every time an actor steps on a set wagon, it moves. Are there special casters that are used in the theater that won't swivel or roll until they are pushed or pulled?

A. If you can drill a hole in the stage, you can use regular swivel casters, but attach two sliding barrel bolts to the upstage side of the wagon, one at either end. The bolt slides down into a hole in the stage floor, anchoring the wagon. (The hole needs to be only slightly larger than the diameter of the bolt.) When the time comes for the wagon to be moved, you slide the bolt up and lock it to one side and out of the hole. The wagon then can be moved easily.

You also can use locking casters. Most of these have a simple side-step brake on the side, operated by foot pressure. You push down on one side of the brake lever to stop the caster, and on the other side to release the brake. Normally, you need only use these casters on the upstage corners of the wagon. The other casters on the unit can be normal swivel casters.

You should be able to find side-step casters and barrel bolts at a large hardware store or hardware superstore.

Q. Our smallish community theater company (and several other performing-arts groups) rents a local performing-arts facility. There is an issue about whether user groups should be able to stabilize sets by screwing, nailing, or bolting set pieces to the floor. Can you suggest any solution?

A. We can understand why a public facility might consider such a policy. Each screw, bolt, or nail that goes into a wood floor leaves a hole when removed. Over time, the smooth surface will disintegrate and need to be replaced.

On the other hand, sets must be securely anchored to be safe. Thus, it's our opinion that damage to the floor should be treated as a part of normal wear and tear. Floor-replacement cost can be built into the budget (and rental fee). This is the most sensible approach when there is a subfloor of strong wood, overlaid with Masonite or a similar composite surface. The surface takes the brunt of the punishment and is removed every three to four years (along with ten to fifteen coats of paint!). The wood underneath is sanded smooth and new Masonite is laid on top and secured with inset screws. We know of one community facility, built in 1973, that has used this method without any problems. The stage subflooring is in excellent condition, the manager tells us, and groups using the stage are required to fill all holes after striking the set.

Some facilities do ban using nails in the floor because they break the wood fibers going in and tear them when pulled out. Screws cause less damage and can provide a more secure anchor.

If your facility decides to ban the use of nails or screws in the floor, you have several options. One is to anchor set pieces by means of a triangular brace attached at right angles to the back; the part of the brace that rests on the floor is then weighted with a heavy pig (iron bar) or sandbag. Another option is to design sets to rest on a series of 4-footx8-footx4-inch platforms. In this way, all screws go into the platform, not the stage floor. (Note: The platforms should be bolted together so their combined mass will support tall or heavy units.)

Q. Occasionally we've miscalculated on the amount needed of a special color and the mix begins to run out before all the flats have been covered. Is there a way to survive this without having to go back, mix a new, larger batch and repaint the entire set when we're about ready to open?

A. If you have just one straight wall, you will probably have to repaint, although you can try the following: Before you run out of the original paint, mix it half and half with the new batch. Use the mixture to bridge the two colors. On the other hand, if your set has angles (such as a box set), go back and repaint so that the two mix at the corner; differences in color are much less noticeable at such points.

38 | *Did You Know?*

Color Trick

According to the folks at Lee Filters, if you suffer burnout problems with saturated colors during the run of a show, you may be able to substitute another color to create the same effect. Choose another gel of similar color but lighter density (that is, less saturated). When you put this replacement color in your instrument, reduce the light's intensity to about 70 to 80 percent of what it was. This will produce approximately the same color effect, Lee says, but the gel will not burn out as quickly as it did using the darker color.

Getting Attached

Using nails to attach flats to one another (or anything else) is at best a temporary solution. Constant use will eventually weaken the wood. Try to use nails only when it's essential and not as a replacement for screws, hinges, or lash hardware. Your flat frames will last longer and remain stronger without any nails at all. More important, perhaps, is that last-minute changes during technical rehearsal (or even performance) will go more smoothly if you use the right fasteners.

Seeing the Light

Two types of lighting fixtures make it easy to illuminate light control panels, rack sound equipment, the stage manager, prop tables, or other small workspaces back stage. The Keyboard Light™ and the Grippy™ from Pleamonn Products provide cool, uniform illumination with minimal obstruction of vision or physical access.

Each fixture is essentially a $\frac{7}{8}$-inch tube containing a cool, long-lived fluorescent lamp, in both 9- and 12-inch lengths. The 8-watt 12-inch lamp produces the light of a 60-watt incandescent bulb, has a 10,000-hour life, and can be replaced reasonably inexpensively. The fluorescent tube is mounted in a thermoplastic reflector that can be rotated 180 degrees in either direction, effectively directing the light where needed. The lamp is mounted on a 9-inch gooseneck, terminating in a threaded connector that allows it to fit the wide array of mounting accessories offered by the manufacturer.

The Keyboard Light, in side- and rear-mount versions, is best for use in control booths, a table or desk mounting, or anywhere you need even, portable, glare-free light. The Grippy version meets a need created by the growing use of computers in the theater. It requires no desk space and fits into a set of self-adhesive mounting clips. A swivel ball joint allows the light to be positioned over the keyboard or workspace.

Beware the Shortcut

Sometimes during the rush to get a show ready, technical staff take shortcuts that can cause real problems for a theater's lighting system. For example, most systems suffer significantly from having loads patched or plugged into the dimmer while the dimmer is on and its control channel is reading more than zero. This is referred to as "hot-patching," and the resulting arcing damages the components of the patch system.

Another problem is overloading, which occurs when there is no proper documentation on what load is in each circuit. Accidentally patching too many instruments onto one dimmer will trip the circuit breaker or other over-current protection device. In newer setups this may cause a momentary inconvenience, but remember that as circuit breakers age they begin to fail under smaller loads and should be replaced. Bypassing an over-current protection in any way can lead to serious damage to your equipment—or a fire.

Keep It Simple

When rehanging or refocusing lights, it's often difficult to make yourself heard by either the supervisor below or the technician above. This is especially true if there are others in the theater who are also talking, hammering, or whatever. Keep directions simple. Even an inexperienced electrician can focus if he is given clear, intelligent instructions like "up," "down," "left," "right," "bigger," and "smaller." Plus, the person giving the orders reduces the likelihood of developing laryngitis from shouting complex instructions.

Putting Them Away

If you save platforms and stair units, store them with any padding or canvas covering intact—when you use them again, this ready-to-use covering could come in handy.

Making Your Mark

If you have to make pencil marks on finished scenery (to show where hinges or other items are to be installed), press a piece of masking tape into place at the spot where the mark is to be made. Then pencil directly onto the tape. When you're done, the tape can be removed without damaging the paint.

Hands Off

Make sure that stagehands know that they are not to shift sets unless they have had prior briefing. Often, sets are complex and potentially fragile. In other cases, rigging or drapes may be torn by someone who doesn't understand the steps that must be taken before shifting.

PROPS

*P*roperties, or props, are much more than objects for
actors to hold. They often are essential to the sense
of a scene, or help an actor create and maintain a
character. Actors depend on props being in place and
in working order before they use them. It's essential, then, to
have the right ones back stage, keep them organized, and always make sure they are at the ready.

39 | *When You Have to Borrow*

Getting Props and Keeping Them Safe

*I*f you can't make or buy a prop, you'll have to borrow it. Persuading someone to loan something of value requires some preparation, as well as courtesy and tact. Here are some guidelines to help get what you need and build rapport with the lender so you can ask again at some time in the future.

1. *Know exactly what you want.* You're more likely to get cooperation if you approach someone with a list of specifics. It shows organization and seriousness of purpose. It also indicates a certain level of responsibility.

2. However, *have a list of alternatives in mind* in case a source is willing to loan items but doesn't have the specific items you're seeking. For example, a florist shop might not have an art deco vase, but could offer a silk flower arrangement to put in the one you eventually find.

3. If you're borrowing from a store, *be sure to ask permission from the owner or manager*, not a clerk. If borrowing from an individual, ask the actual owner of the item.

4. *Don't ask to borrow something unless you really need it.* Lenders want to know that they are contributing to the success of your production.

5. *Make sure whoever represents your theater in this process has the authority to negotiate for a loan* and take responsibility for the borrowed item.

6. *Be honest with the person from whom you're borrowing.* Let the person know the possibility of damage, but also the care you'll give the items and the responsibility for damage and loss your theater will assume.

7. *Set dates and times for the pickup and return of the items*—and honor them.

8. *Create a loan-agreement form* and fill it out for each item. The form should include the following:

a. The condition of the item when it was loaned, noting any scratches, dents, and any other damages. The owner should initial this information as acknowledgment of their existence at the time of the loan.

b. The current value of the item, as agreed to by the owner and the borrower. This will become the basis for repayment if the item is lost or damaged.

c. Who shall be responsible for transporting the item to the theater. A merchant may prefer to take this responsibility, since the item will be handled by an employee who is familiar with the item, and thus better able to ensure its safety.

d. The location of the theater where the item will be used.

e. The names and phone numbers of the lender and of the borrower representing the theater.

f. The date and time the item is to be returned.

g. A space to acknowledge return of the item with a statement of the condition when returned.

9. *Offer some kind of compensation* for the loan, such as complimentary tickets or acknowledgment in the program or both. This, plus the safe and timely return of the item, should help you the next time you ask.

10. If an item in your care is damaged during the production, *have a plan on how to offer restitution*. Never borrow a one-of-a-kind or historical item that can't be replaced. Antiques are lovely and can add authenticity to a scene, but if something is easily damaged, it shouldn't be on stage.

40 Working with Weapons

While you need to take care of all your props, weapons demand an even higher level of attention. Even if they are being used in a different manner than was intended, they still can be dangerous—on stage and back stage.

Advice on How to Use Them Correctly— and Safely

Eileen P. Duggan

Weapons used for theatrical purposes are still weapons, says fight director Michael Monsey, and should be treated with the utmost respect.

Monsey maintains an extensive collection of weapons and related items, including a rapier, switchblades, whips, chains, various knives, quarterstaffs (6-foot pieces of wood used in medieval times), rubber clubs, leather gloves, sheaths for swords and knives, and cheap revolvers in various sizes. Over the years, he has developed a number of rules when working with all those weapons. While actors frequently are instructed about how to deal with weapons, Monsey here offers some rules worded for the benefit of stage managers and prop persons:

■ Use only stage combat swords and knives whose edges have been blunted. But even so, remember they are still sharp enough to hurt someone.

■ Swords should be sturdy enough to take thousands of blows. Stage combat swords are balanced properly for parrying and thrusting.

■ A variety of broadswords, small swords, rapiers, maces, and battle-axes can be rented through a few specialized companies. Although costume shops rent or sell show swords that can be worn, they should not be used in stage combat. Real swords should never be used because they're sharp and will break.

■ Keep all knives and swords in sheaths when not in use.

■ Real revolvers in .22, .32, .44, and .45 calibers can be used with proper blank ammunition. Gun stores can provide custom blank ammunition to fit the sound level you need.

■ "Guns and high schools don't go together," Monsey says. High school productions should use a track and field starting pistol, or an adult should take charge of the gun, bringing it to and from every performance. Guns should be present on the premises only during show time and not stored at a high school. "And I don't use guns in junior highs at all," Monsey says.

■ Modified semiautomatic or automatic weapons can be obtained from several gun dealers around the country. However, someone in the show must have special licensing to possess these weapons. Special ammunition is available "and it's very, very expensive," Monsey says.

■ If you plan to rent firearms, make sure to check applicable local, state, and federal laws. "And each rental company will have its own rules concerning the sale, rental, and transporting of firearms," Monsey says.

Gun Control

If your play calls for a gun to be used, your first concern must be safety. Here are some tips on firearm safety from Stembridge Gun Rentals, of Glendale, California, which rents firearms to theater and film productions.

Giving instruction in the proper and safe use of firearms is the responsibility of the property master. The property master is responsible for *all* guns during production; there also may be a hired weapons specialist on the set.

The prop master should not issue a firearm to anyone without first determining that that person is knowledgeable in its use. Knowledge of operating features and safety devices on a gun, as well as the precautions to be taken in handling it, are prerequisites to issuing weapons.

Loading of weapons and magazines will be done by the prop master or by experienced people working under his or her supervision. Keep the gun's safety on until just before the weapon is to work. At the end of a scene, guns should be unloaded and checked to be certain they are empty of blanks. Do an inventory whenever guns have been issued to be sure of their return. Weapons should be cleaned, checked, and inventoried at the end of each day.

Treat firearms with care; do not lay a gun down in such a way that dirt can clog the barrel or that parts can be damaged. Do not fire any weapon that is clogged with any material. No one should modify any firearm; in case of malfunction, the correction should be made by someone qualified to handle it, or the weapon returned to the rental house.

Here are some other rules:

- Never bring live ammunition to the theater.
- Do not allow any personal firearms to be brought on the set.
- Never point a firearm at anyone, including yourself.
- *No one* ever should engage in horseplay with a firearm.
- Do not fire a blank within 20 feet of anyone; some blanks call for even longer distances. A quarter-load blank is as much a potential hazard as a full-load blank; there is still a wad that is fragmented upon firing.

Everything in Its Place

41

A Simple Way to Keep Track of What's There— and Isn't

F ew things are as maddening to the prop person as an absent prop at the end of a performance. Here's an easy way to know what's missing and who had it last.

Cover your prop table with a vinyl tablecloth, which is sold as large as 60×102 inches. If the show has many props and your table is large, buy vinyl tablecloth by the roll, which is sold at some party stores for as little as 60 cents a yard. You can use a painter's drop cloth, but you'll get better results if the vinyl is opaque rather than transparent.

On the day you set up shop backstage, place each prop on the vinyl-covered table in the approximate order in which it will be needed. (Save some room for items added at the last minute.) Using a grease pencil or felt marking pen, draw around each prop, making an outline of it. (If the item is too small to make this practical, draw an enlarged version of the outline.)

Remove the props and label each outline with the name of the item, the actor who uses it, and the act and scene in which it is used on stage. For example: "Book/Franklin, Act III/2." When you're done with the labeling, replace each prop on its outline.

Make sure the cast knows whether props are to be replaced by them or given to a prop assistant to be put back on the table.

The advantage to this system is that you and the actors know immediately where to find an item, and can check before the show begins to make sure all props are in place. If the prop person is absent for some reason, or an understudy is playing the role, it is still easy enough to determine the readiness of all props.

At the end of the run, the vinyl table covering can be tossed or saved for use as a drop cloth.

42 | *Keeping Track*

Of course, it is essential to know where all your props are—not just the ones used in the last performance. This is, by definition, a much greater undertaking, but essential to the long-term health of your operation.

A Spreadsheet Is an Easy, Versatile Way to Keep Track of Everything You Use

GEORGE F. LEDO

*I*t's an ongoing problems all companies face: How to keep track of the hundreds—or thousands—of props that have collected over the years and that will continue to accumulate? Unfortunately, the usual inventory systems, such as a card index, a loose-leaf binder, or a photo album, are so time-consuming to maintain that they often fall into disuse. A computerized system sounds like a great idea, but many people assume it's more trouble than it's worth.

So what to do?

You *can* set up a simple and effective props-inventory system on a computer, but there's a secret. It's a type of program that is commonly available in any number of variations, is very easy to use, and requires absolutely no programming—it's called a *spreadsheet.*

What It Is

A spreadsheet is nothing more than one of those old ruled pads used by accountants, with lines and columns, that allows you to enter different types of information (not just numbers) and to keep everything organized. The beauty of using a computer spreadsheet, however, is that you can change anything at a moment's notice: the information is always there and you can do with it as you will. Anytime.

Other types of programs, such as databases, may be more suitable for maintaining an extensive inventory because they let you create entry forms, detailed reports, and other goodies. However, for ease of learning and simplicity of operation, a spreadsheet (such as Microsoft Excel™) can't be beat.

Design the System

Since you want to keep this system simple and easy to use, start by limiting the amount of information collected on each prop to just a few things:

What It Is. ■ The item can be a radio, a lamp, a telephone, a sword, or anything else. This is what the director or the script asks for. Most items can be referred to in one or two words.

A General Description. ■ Once you know what the item is, you can describe it in just a few more words. In the case of a telephone, it could be a push-button desk model, a rotary dial, a wall-mounted phone, or even an old-fashioned candlestick-style. Give just enough of a description for the director or head of props to know if it's useable.

A Note or Two. ■ Does the phone work? What color is it? Is the statue missing an arm? Is the sword blade bent? Again, two or three words are usually enough.

What Play the Prop Was Last Used In. ■ This provides a clue to the overall look and feel of the prop. You can imagine, for example, that a telephone used in *Who's Afraid of Virginia Woolf?* would be different from one used in a stage version of *Life with Father*.

Cost. ■ Who remembers the price of that imitation Tiffany lamp bought three years ago? This information will come in handy later, so keep it for now.

Current. ■ This indicates those items used in the current production. Simply mark the item with an X.

Tag or Inventory Number. ■ This will help ensure there's no mistake about whether that clock on the mantel is the one you want. For our purposes, don't bother setting up a classification system; simply start with "1" and go on from there. You can use your company's initials in front of the number. If the name is Poorhouse Players, label the props PHP1, PHP2, and so on.

This system provides seven pieces of information on each prop, all in plain English.

Set It Up

A spreadsheet program lets you change anything, even after you've entered several thousand pieces of information. You can add lines or columns in the middle of the sheet (try doing that on the old ruled pad!), get rid of lines or columns, and move things around. And it only takes a moment. Thus, if you come up with other ideas after using this system for a few months, you can make changes without having to retype everything. And you can even transfer it all to many database programs and create your own entry forms and detailed reports.

Some columns are wider than others; you can change the width of any column anytime. If you don't know something about a prop (such as how much it cost), you can leave it blank and fill it in later.

You can enter the information into the computer in one of two ways. Go to the prop room, write down everything on a pad, and then type it in. Or take along a laptop computer—if one's available—and save yourself a lot of time, questions, and double-checking. (It can even be someone else's laptop—you always can transfer the information to your own computer later.)

Using It

The easiest way to set up this system is to assign sequential numbers to the props. That way swords are mixed in with lamps, chairs, books, and radios. If you print out this kind of list as is, you get a simple inventory with props listed in order of tag number.

But you can *sort* the list according to what's in Column B, which gives you all the items in alphabetical order, starting with a book, then a calculator, and so on. The tag numbers are now scrambled, but each number still corresponds to the correct prop. You can print this to get an alphabetized inventory, which makes things much easier to find (at least on paper). By the way, you also can sort on two or more columns at the same time. If you do this, you could, for instance, alphabetize the item names and the descriptions.

Next we'll pick out a few items for our current production, which we'll call *Spelvin*. Column G can be the current show column, and you can mark those items to be used with an X. Sort the entire list based on the information in Column G, and now the items you want to use for *Spelvin* are at the top.

Well, maybe not all the items. What if you have to purchase some more items—let's say two candlesticks, a serving cart, and a plant? So you go shopping and come back with the stuff. Here's where this system really begins to earn its keep.

You go to the bottom of the complete inventory and begin entering the new items, starting with the candlesticks. Write *Spelvin* in the "Last Used" column, enter the cost in Column F, and put the X under "Current." Now tell the computer to print out just these three new items (with the prices added up), and out comes a report that you can hand in with the receipts to get reimbursed. (Your manual will show you how to add the figures.)

Sort the current items in column G and you'll get all the props you want for *Spelvin*, including the candlesticks, cart, and plant, which are at the top of the list. After the show, you can go back and change the applicable show names in the "Last Used" column to *Spelvin* so the inventory will be up to date.

Other Uses for the System

If your theater loans or rents props to other groups, you can print out a list of what they took and send it along as a reminder or as an invoice. You may want to add columns to indicate who borrowed it and when. Most programs let you "hide" the columns you don't want borrowers to see. If the other group wants to see what radios you have, you can print out a list showing just the radios. If somebody donates materials to your company, you can print out a list for them. Or if you store your props in more than one location, you can add a column to show each prop's location.

The same system can be used for lighting instruments, scenery pieces, or even costumes. The uses are practically endless, yet the system is very easy to set up and maintain.

Affixing Serial Numbers

Since labels can fall off and wired tags can be removed or get torn, one of the best ways to tag an item is to borrow an idea from museums: write the number right on the prop.

Most museums paint a small white spot on the bottom of the item and then write the number on the paint with a black ink pen.

The number doesn't have to be very large—just big enough to be legible. With museums, it's a consistent method and all employees are familiar with it, so it works fine.

First set up some guidelines everyone will follow. For instance, the label may be on the bottom of all items that sit on a table, but under the left front corner of a table or chair, and in the middle of the back of a framed picture. Keep it simple, but make it consistent.

Next, standardize the size of the paint spot. A spot about the size of a penny is usually enough, and it won't be noticed from the audience. Make sure to clean or sand the area where the paint will go and use a flat oil-based paint (not a latex). If the prop is white or light-colored, paint a black spot on it first and then, inside it, the white spot; that way there's a border on the white and everyone will recognize it as your standard label.

Put the number on with a black ballpoint pen or, better yet, with a drafting pen. This type of ink doesn't fade or smear like some markers do. If you want to, you can spray a little clear acrylic on top to protect it.

When You Run Out of Room | 43

You need to keep track of all your props, but that becomes a lot harder when you don't have enough space to store them all. Particularly for theater companies that have endured for a long time, storage—for both props and set pieces—becomes an increasingly complicated issue.

How to Find Useable Storage Space at Little or No Cost

George F. Ledo

A t some time you may run out of storage room for scenery, props, or costumes and have to go looking for more space. Your budget, however, may not allow for the additional rent, forcing you to look for donations of space or funds with which to pay for the space. But there is a way to turn the process into an opportunity to increase community interest in your company and generate new business. Here's how to seek—and find—useable space at little or no cost through local businesses.

The Plan of Attack

Before you ask anything of anyone, prepare yourself to answer questions and assure prospects that you are reliable and responsible, and that you know exactly what you need in the way of space.

Local businesses may be interested in helping you, but they probably don't understand how a theatrical company functions. You must be able to respond to some very legitimate concerns, such as safety (Will the stuff be flammable? Will it attract rodents?), security (Who will access the space, and at what hours?), liability, responsibility, and credibility

(Are these people really serious about this?). These are issues that can stop any deal dead in its tracks.

To make a valid decision, the prospects need to know what kind of space you need, how much of it, and for how long. Not being in our business, they may not be aware of some important issues we take for granted, such as keeping the material clean, dry, and accessible. Also, the more they know about what you need, the easier they can figure out what it will cost and whether they can afford it.

Success by Design

In the world of professional sales, the type of concerns listed previously is known as *resistance*—the excuses a prospect makes for not buying something. You must eliminate (or at least reduce) the resistance to your proposal by addressing those concerns before they come up.

Start by getting organized. Take a few pictures of your existing storage space; you'll use these later in a set of "before and after" shots. Next, get ruthless. Set aside anything that will not be used again or that will cost more to repair or repaint than to build or buy. This is usually the hardest part of the project, but it's amazing how much stored material is really junk. Leave it alone for a day or two and then come back to it; review your list and make any necessary changes.

Now get creative: design (not build) a storage system (racks and shelves) for the material you need to keep, and add some space for growth. You may be able to recycle any good lumber for this purpose. Make sure the system can be configured in different ways, since you don't yet know the size and shape of your new space. (While you're at it, figure out how you will use the old space when it becomes available.) Discard, sell, donate, or recycle all the material you won't use again.

Now start networking. Talk to your local school or college drafting instructor, tell him or her about the project, and ask for help drawing up the system in two or three different configurations, making sure to leave enough clear space for at least two people to work comfortably. If this sounds interesting enough, the teacher may assign it as a class project, and maybe even talk to the wood shop class about building it, which could result in an offer to help with construction. Using the drawings, figure out how many square feet you need and how high the space needs to be. (By this time you've met a few new people. Stop for a moment and add them to your company's mailing list.)

Finally, determine how much you can afford to pay for the new space and how you might lower that cost. Consider things such as partial rent, donations of season tickets, a benefit performance, free lessons, and similar items. These are all legitimate trading goods for a nonprofit organization or school.

Address the Concerns

Now that you know everything about the space you'll need, you can start addressing these concerns:

- *Safety*. Again, reduce or eliminate anything that can become a fire hazard or attract pests.
- *Security*. Determine who will need access to the space, at what times, and how that access will be controlled.
- *Liability*. Make sure the storage system is safe to use and that there's enough space to work. Determine who will supervise the crew that uses it. Find out if your company carries insurance and exactly what it covers.
- *Responsibility*. Determine who will be in charge of the space and whose phone number will be on file at the storage location.
- *Credibility*. If you've handled these tasks well, you'll be able to demonstrate your commitment to the project and you'll have established credibility.

Determine Whom to Ask

Before starting the actual search, you'll need to develop a list of prospects. Start with your own mailing list, friends, and business associates; they already know your company. What you're looking for are storage and moving firms or businesses that have warehouses or vacant space, as well as anybody who can refer you to one of these.

A great source of contacts and prospects is your local chamber of commerce. Call them and explain what you're trying to do. Chances are they'll be happy to help, especially when they see how well organized your project is.

Once you have a list of ten to fifteen solid prospects, write each one a short letter. Mention how you obtained their name and tell them about your company and your project. Ask for an appointment to meet with them in person, and say you will follow up with a phone call in a few days. Don't mention pricing or trades yet—keep it simple for now. Include something about your company, such as a good review, picture, or flyer on the upcoming season. Mail the letter to arrive by the middle of the week.

Make Your Case

A few days later, call each prospect to make sure they received the letter and to ask for the appointment. Be sure to approach the prospect with a business project (which it is) instead of asking for charity (which it isn't).

They'll have some questions right away. Go ahead and answer them, but your primary goal now is to make the appointment, not a deal. Tell them you'll only need twenty minutes, which is about right for this type of meeting.

Make every effort to keep the meeting to the twenty minutes, by the way. Tell them about your company, show the sketches and any good reviews or pictures, and get them excited about the project. They may have doubts, but if you've done your homework you'll have most of the answers ready.

If they have space and are willing to let you use it, ask to see it but don't agree to taking it yet, since you'll want to explore other options. You may have to do a bit of negotiating here (offering those season tickets as a trade), but keep it simple; you may need to come back for a second round.

If they can offer no help, ask for a referral or two—someone they know who may be willing to talk with you. Most people will be happy to give you a referral, and you will have another name for your contact list. Whether they say yes, maybe, or no, be sure to write them a short thank-you note afterwards; these notes go a long way. And don't forget to add all of these people to your mailing list.

Once you've looked at a few spaces and selected the best one, it's time to go back for the final round of negotiations. Trade those tickets or that benefit performance, offer a free ad in your program, and get the entire agreement in writing. Send every other company that offered space a short note, tell them you selected someone else, and thank them for their help.

Move in and Tell the World

Go ahead then and build your storage system, move your materials, get it all organized, and take some more photographs—the "after" shots. (By the way, you can use the same networking ideas listed previously for help with the actual move.)

Now that you have your space, let the world know what you've accomplished. Either write a press release or simply pick up the phone and call the local newspaper. Better yet, do some more networking: ask your contacts if they know someone at the paper or a television station and if they'd be willing to introduce you.

When you've found an interested reporter, call the company that donated the space and tell them about the press coverage; it's common courtesy. They also may (or may not) want to be interviewed. During the interview, talk about why you need new space, what you plan to do with the old space, and about the company in general. Show the "before and after" pictures or take the reporter on a tour. People love to read this type of story: it's a refreshing change from wars and disasters. Make sure to add the reporter to your mailing list.

So, you've gotten new storage space, lots of new contacts, and free publicity. When you're ready to advertise your next production, call some of your contacts and ask if you can put up a poster at their location. If you made a good impression, they'll be happy to let you do so, and may even buy tickets!

44 | Did You Know?

It Doesn't Hurt to Ask

For its production of *Rumors*, set in an upscale New York home, the Renton (Washington) Community Players managed a donation of an entire coordinated set of furniture. The head of the production crew sent letters to furniture stores in the area asking for help in exchange for complimentary tickets and an advertisement in the program. The manager of a local furniture-rental firm responded with tables, chairs, a sofa, bar, and other elegant pieces—and they delivered and picked up as well.

In a Pinch

Cellulose sponges make good rehearsal props to represent any number of small items. They are lightweight, washable, and come in many different sizes.

The Stage Manager's Role

The stage manager should create a prop list that goes beyond the one printed at the back of the script and includes the props actually being used. The SM doesn't create the list, but should maintain a complete one from the props master. The SM must know to whom each prop is assigned and its offstage location.

The SM also should know if anything has to be done to prepare the prop. Do the glasses have to be washed each night? Do items have to be replaced or refilled for each show? Is the prop rented? From where? Is it loaned? By whom?

Proverbial Wisdom

Some Biblical-sounding proverbs about theater operations have been turning up on the Internet. Two of them are particularly relevant to handling props:

- Do not give actors their props before their time, for surely they shall lose or break them.

- When told the placement of props by the director, do not write these things in ink upon the script, for surely the director shall change his mind.

THE STRIKE

W hen a production has finished its last performance, it is time to dismantle the sets, discard what cannot be saved, and store those pieces that can. The onstage work is done, but the backstage activity heats up. It can be a particularly feverish time back stage because, frequently, the strike has to be accomplished in a short period of time, with some workers eager perhaps to head out the door—and others wanting to head to the strike party. Some set pieces will need to be discarded and some put in storage. Some materials, including costumes, will need to be sent back to rental houses while others will be broken down into their component parts.

For these reasons and because the strike often takes place immediately after the final performance, it is essential to plan carefully to keep things moving efficiently and safely.

45 | Strike While the Iron Is Hot

Dismantling a Production Needs Even More Planning Than Putting One Up

The use of the word *strike*—in the theatrical sense of dismantling a production—was recorded one hundred years ago, although builders used the word as early as the seventeenth century to mean *remove*, and sailors to mean *lower* (a mast or sail) in the fourteenth century.

Today, it is usual to strike a set directly after the final performance, and there is good reason for doing so—a full complement of workers, both cast and crew. It's our experience that workers show remarkable energy during strike, and it might as well be harnessed immediately.

However, this energy has its down side. Unless the strike is planned and supervised, some participants may end up destroying valuable materials in their enthusiasm. Also, working conditions often are chaotic at best. We have seen inexperienced workers step on nails, drive splinters into their hands, hit fellow workers on the head with boards, and accidentally knock holes in material that was to be salvaged for reuse.

Who's in Charge Here?

One person should be assigned responsibility for running the strike. This can be—and often is—the stage manager, but also may be the head carpenter or builder. This person should *not* do any of the actual work, but should be positioned in a central place and make the work assignments and direct the proceedings. He or she must make sure that units to be saved aren't torn up, that hardware is removed and stored properly, that the stage is returned to its original condition, and that work is carried on safely. Here is an overview of what should take place.

Ideally, work assignments should be made prior to the strike. The organizer should break down the tasks and determine how many people are needed for each one. Then the cast and crew should sign up themselves or be assigned tasks. Before strike begins, explain to the workers just what is to be saved and how. Have storage containers for hardware and make sure they are clearly marked, or have workers bring hardware to one place and assign someone to stay there and sort it into the appropriate containers.

Order of Business

Before the curtain falls for the final time, all equipment needed for the strike should be ready for use. Some companies have enough to go around; others ask cast and crew to bring their own. Screwdrivers, wrenches, crowbars, and claw hammers are most useful. Tell workers to write their names on any tools they bring—tools look alike. Have as many large trash containers available as possible; a dumpster is particularly useful if you have a waste-removal service that provides these large containers.

The basic order for a strike is the reverse of setup. Remove furniture and loose decorative pieces first. If a ceiling flat has been used, it goes next. Platforms and stair units follow. Architectural units attached to wall units then are removed, followed by all but essential wall supports. The next step is to "walk" the wall units down to the floor and disassemble them.

Which materials should be saved and which thrown out? This depends in great part on the amount of storage space you have and how well organized it is. It's our experience that many theater companies save too much so that material piles up so deeply in storage that it is easier to buy new material than to hunt through the debris for reusable pieces. It is better to organize your storage area carefully so you can keep less and use it more. How you build your sets also influences how much can be saved. Nails, for example, are easy to drive in, but difficult to remove quickly without damaging the wood. Some groups bolt all set pieces together, using drill attachments. At the end of shows, all basic structural pieces are saved by removing the bolts and stacking the essential framing lumber, stairs, and platforms. This saves a great deal of money in the process. It also creates a less chaotic strike: since people know that everything is to be saved, they tend to work more carefully.

46 | Stage Struck
The Safe Way to Take Down a Show

ELBIN CLEVELAND

The strike of a show can be an especially dangerous time. It's when several production departments must operate on stage simultaneously and when people can get a little crazy about demolishing everything in sight quickly so they won't miss any of the strike party.

Planning for strike should begin at the same time as planning for the production and should be an integral part of the process. Take scenery as an example: it is often the most complicated element and the most time-consuming to strike. As the scenery is designed, consider its construction. Perhaps you can use stock scenery items that will be salvaged for post-production storage and future reuse. If new scenic items must be constructed, try to incorporate new stock units that can be salvaged later to increase your useful inventory of scenic pieces.

Always consider which fastener or joining methods will provide secure construction and still facilitate strike. Don't use glue except for building new stock units unless it's really necessary. Glued materials are very difficult—and often impossible—to strike. Use duplex (double-headed) scaffold nails or screws and bolts instead of common nails wherever possible; even better, use loose-pin hinges, hasps, or roto-locks. Best of all, use various clamps (C-clamps, bar clamps, web clamps) to join scenic units. Clamps require no hardware, are adjustable, and come off quickly for strike—and they last forever.

Consult regularly with other production departments during the construction process. That way you can plan for the efficient laying and strike of sound and light cables, the timely removal of stage props, and the safe disposition of rigged and flown units.

Put It Down on Paper

If you haven't had time to actually plan the strike before the show opens—and who does?—then use the performance days to do so. Use an outline form and write down the major areas to be handled during the strike: scenery, lighting, props, and so on. (Once you have the basic form in your computer, you can reuse it for every show with only minor modifications.)

Then write down the major elements of each area. For scenery, this might include the following: flat work, flown scenery, platforms, mechanical elements, escape units, and masking. Subdivide these into particular components for the particular show, and note any special problems that may be associated with the strike of any part. If you hadn't planned the construction for easy dismantling, you must work harder now.

Review the construction drawings so you don't forget anything. Also, walk the set to refresh your memory of construction and to note any changes between the plans and the reality. Look at all the details; careful observation here will save time and reduce hazards later.

Next, flesh out the outline you have been preparing. Rearrange and supplement or delete as necessary. Check with other production areas to confirm that you have included everything from the fall of the final curtain to the closing and locking of the load-out door.

Picture It

When you believe the outline is complete, find a quiet time to sit down and visualize the progress of the strike. This is a critical step, so give it your full effort. Imagine every task that is required during strike and the execution of those tasks. Carefully consider how many people are necessary to safely perform each task. Estimate the time required for each operation by every strike worker. Imagine which tasks can occur simultaneously and determine which ones must be sequential. Mentally divide the available workspace into separate areas for stripping hardware, denailing, and stacking completed work.

Visualize the "choreography" of the entire strike movement by movement. How can one *pas de deux* (work done by two people) occur at the same time without interfering with another *pas de quatre* (work done by four people)? Which tasks require many people and which can be done by only one? All this may sound very time-consuming, and the first time you do it, that may actually be true. However, the same way your experience enables you to plan for safe and efficient construction, your experience here will soon enable you to plan for safe and efficient strike. The more you do it, the better and the quicker you will become.

When you feel comfortable with your "choreographic composition," begin casting the players for the various "performance roles." Obviously, the most experienced individuals should head each crew. Then individual teams can be assigned to each task on your outline. Be sure each team has at least one trained or experienced person to guide the other workers.

If you have done your work early enough, you should put your plan aside for a day or so. This "setting time" is an important but often overlooked part of any creative effort. When you return to the project in a day or two, your mind will be fresh. You easily will spot any errors and you may have even better ideas than before.

Finally, write all this down in a coherent plan, easily understood by the workers. Your objective should be the same as it was for the construction phase: the instructions should be so clear that the work can proceed safely even in your absence. Prepare several copies of your outline and sequential plan. Give one to each crew head two or three days before strike. Post another back stage. This will show others that your strike is a carefully planned operation, not a haphazard free-for-all. It also will give many folks the opportunity to identify any errors or omissions you may have made.

Now make a sequential list of tasks for each team. Print out a copy for each crew head and team leader. Have these ready before strike night. These worksheets will guide each worker through a safe and efficient strike.

Before strike, meet with all crew heads and as many workers as possible. Explain the plan step by step. Emphasize "choreographic thinking." Specify how to avoid dangerous situations and insist on cautious behavior. The single most important factor in safety is a safety-conscious attitude; tolerate nothing less.

During strike, supervise the entire scene intently. Observe the progress of each team and adjust the sequence of tasks as required by reality. Some community theater companies rely on actors, out of makeup and costume, to help with strike. Remember that actors are often weary after performance, and fatigue can bring on injuries—to themselves, other members of the crew, or the set pieces. If this is done at your company, assign actors to work with someone who is experienced and who can instruct them.

Despite the wishes of your workers, this is not the time to play loud rock music. The noise makes commands and other sounds harder to hear, while the tempo and theme are absolutely contrary to the energetic but methodical "performances" you want. Instead, play peaceful classical instrumental music. These sounds naturally slow people down and promote smooth operation. (If this music is not commonly played in your scene studio, consider changing to it. It has the same positive effect during construction, and can be good education if you work with students.)

Finally, practice some "Monday morning quarterbacking." Review the strike with your colleagues to find out why some plans didn't work as intended. Your next strike will be even better.

Ten Tips

1. Have a fully stocked first-aid kit onsite.

2. Everyone on stage must wear a hardhat and other personal protective equipment such as work gloves and face masks.

3. Strike can be dusty and dirty. If so, provide all workers with fiber dust masks.

4. Everyone must understand that efficient use of the time, not unbridled haste, is the objective.

5. All tools, dollies, hand trucks, ladders, and other equipment must be prechecked for safety and preplaced for efficiency.

6. Have assorted refuse containers preplaced and clearly marked.

7. Do not permit workers to toss each other tools. This dangerous practice encourages people to toss other things. Have enough tools for everyone.

8. Never permit counterweight unloading unless the stage is totally clear of personnel.

9. Take regular 10-minute breaks every hour.

10. Even the most complicated strike should halt after 4 hours. Take a full meal break and then continue—or stop until the next day.

47 | *Talking It Over*
After a Show Closes, Review What Went Right and Wrong—and Why

Apost-production meeting, or "postmortem," called by the stage manager and including technicians, designers, managers, and stage crew, can be a powerful tool in improving your productions. Since the show, with all its problems and successes, is still very much alive in the memory, this is an ideal time to review how well things are running back stage, which procedures need to be changed, and which need to be kept and improved.

Christopher James, who runs the Fully Reciprocal Theater Company in Minneapolis, is typical of those who praise postmortems. "They help us evaluate our successes and failures, and give people a chance to reflect upon their experiences with a clearer perspective than when they were rushing to meet opening-night deadlines. The problem is, as much as we support postmortems in theory, they're very hard to actually arrange. It seems like about a week after closing is the ideal time for a postmortem, but by that point, actors and technicians are busy doing all the things they didn't do while they were working on the production. This is especially hard for smaller theaters that pay actors and technicians smaller stipends, or for theaters that rely on volunteers. In these situations, people aren't willing to sacrifice yet another evening for a postmortem. But when they do happen, they're instructive and enlightening, and they help a cast and crew with closure on the project, which is also important."

The need for closure can be a powerful motivator in making a postmortem a productive experience, according to Robin Share, of Sherman Oaks, California. Share has taught theater for more than a dozen years at the high school and college level, and served as Resident Director for Actors Alley Repertory Theater. While teaching at a performing-arts high school, she worked with the same ensemble of performance students for a full year, for five or six productions.

"After each production we always had a full and organized post-mortem, usually the Tuesday after closing, in the form of a mini-retreat," she explains. "These were always very structured, and very, very constructive, because the conclusions we reached were then turned into recommendations to be implemented in the next production. After the last show of the year we had a meeting that was more a celebration than a reflection. I've never had as satisfying or successful experiences in terms of a company growing together as I did during those years."

A Learning Experience

Not surprisingly, most of those we heard from on this subject were involved with academic theater. One reason, as pointed out by Charmi Zoll, a graduate student at the University of Waterloo in Ontario, Canada, is that "the academic environment practically demands postmortems. We are a learning institution, after all, and you can't easily learn from your mistakes if they aren't recognized. Our postmortems have been instrumental in troubleshooting and smooth production planning," Zoll adds. "When all is said and done, they are indispensable."

Some universities take a different approach. At Harvard, according to resident designer Dan Scully, "we usually don't have postmortems (unless you count strike parties, where you remember everything that screwed up). What we do have is the—drum roll—Theater Summit. The heads of the major drama organizations, along with dance organizations, college officers, and anyone else who is interested, gather to discuss the state of Harvard theater and how to improve it. Because we have no drama department overseeing all the shows, this helps us organize and synchronize all the many people doing shows. Topics discussed at the last summit ranged from storage space for scenery and props to setting up a royalties fund, and also forming a production staff for all the dance shows."

A summit meeting, as useful as it is, can't take the place of the postmortem that is held while the memory of a production is still fresh. Harvard aside, one reason postmortems are most common in an academic setting is that student and staff directors, designers, and technicians normally don't leave when the show closes. But many community, regional, and summer theaters also use the same production staff each season. With some effective planning, postmortems can be made part of almost any production schedule.

The Informal Approach

Don Picket, of Raleigh, North Carolina, recalls that "many years ago these postmortem sessions were a fact of life when doing a short-term show in established theaters. I sat through many. I think they still happen, but not as formally anymore."

Chip Bernard, lighting director for Fourquest Entertainment in Seminole, Florida, agrees that postmortems these days are often informal. "I have worked in summer-stock organizations where, during the first meeting on the next show, the previous show was discussed. Also, working on tour, the crew will usually have the after load-out bus chat to discuss the day's events and to touch base on the next venue."

Also favoring a mix of formal and informal is Stephen Mayotte, of Mayotte Mobile Stage Lighting in North Chelmsford, Massachusetts. "We don't wait until the show is completed," he explains. "The load-in and rehearsals get special attention. When the show is over, the performances and the load-out are reviewed. But I keep detailed notes on every show. The goals—of course—are to be quicker, safer, smarter, and better. It works. When you learn from the past, mistakes aren't repeated. I can trace specialized carts, jigs, cables—— you name it—to postmortems."

A Sense of Trust

As Robin Share points out, the key to a successful postmortem is a clear sense of purpose and a set of procedural rules. There also needs to be a strong sense of trust.

William Esty, a master carpenter in North Lauderdale, Florida, cites the excellent postmortems at the Coconut Grove Playhouse, where he once worked. "The technical director would start the meeting with a discussion on everything that worked well and why it did. He then moved on to things that did not work well and why. In attendance were carpenters, painters, the assistant technical director, interns, and all shop staff. There was no blame for things that did not work, and there was recognition for those who resolved problems well."

Like Robin Share, Esty believes the well-run postmortem can be a real morale-booster. "This transfer of information is crucial to close the communication gap that exists in many theaters. Everyone benefits from the free flow of information and ideas. It puts a stop to bad habits and eliminates repeated mistakes, saving time and money in the future—not to mention frustration."

However, Esty now works at a different theater, whose technical director is "loathe to implement postmortems for fear of possible negative input. Clearly, it is important that there be an impartial moderator present at any postmortem discussion. This reduces the possibility of harsh, excessive, nonproductive discourse that ultimately will result in bruised egos and low morale."

The possibility that the postmortem will deteriorate into complaints is a real one. Lisa Newman, a freelance lighting director and master electrician in Tempe, Arizona, recalls post-production meetings as an undergraduate that were "glorified bitch sessions that did no good other than make all participants angry and frustrated."

She recalls one in particular, for a musical, that was held a week after strike. "Everyone was required to attend: actors, technicians, musicians, the director, and designers. The meeting started out with the problems the box office had—and there were some big problems. The house/box office manager acknowledged these and said that they were looking into ways to rectify them. Then the female lead complained that the box office had sold the tickets that had been held for her parents. Two hours later, they were still whipping at the box-office mistakes."

In such an environment, there can be no trust, and therefore little hope of a positive outcome. One reason that postmortems often deteriorate into complaint sessions is that too many people are involved. "For this to be an effective meeting," says Chip Bernard, "it must involve a small group of people—perhaps just department heads and creative staff."

One way to improve the outcome is to combine the postmortem with some form of written evaluation, says Linda Eisenstein, who served as director of the Cleveland Public Theater's Festival of New Plays for nearly a decade. "At CPT, we had a small corps of staff and a zillion semitransient artists coming in and out, like Grand Central Station. Without postmortems and evaluations, we wouldn't be able to adjust to changing conditions and faces all the time."

CPT made extensive use of post-production meetings for its annual new-plays festival. "It was such a big event," Eisenstein explains, "with ten to fifteen plays in staged readings over three weeks, twelve different directors, twelve playwrights, discussion leaders, and scores of actors, that we always wanted feedback on what worked or didn't.

"Besides the sit-around-and-talk postmortem," she says, "I had a detailed evaluation form that we circulated to everybody. Based on all that information, we made changes over the years—some radical, most gradual—that made for better productions and smoother administration, with virtually no increase in budget."

The positive experiences cited by Eisenstein and others is proof that the postmortem can be an effective tool in improving a company's productions. The negative experience of some of our respondents serves warning that to be effective, postmortems must be well organized, with clear ground rules, involve a manageable number of people, and lead to observable, positive change.

Did You Know? | *48*

Recycle It

S ave dutchman (cloth that has been soaked in glue) when you strike a set. You'll find that the material works well on older flats, while new or "raw" dutchman works best on new flats.

Some theater companies find that, instead of throwing away set decorations or furniture made for stage use, a well-publicized sale of such items once a year can be a money-maker.

Often you'll find a scrap strip of $\frac{1}{4}$-inch plywood that is 8 feet long and only a few inches wide. Don't throw it away. Instead, use it as a straight edge for drawing lines on other sheets.

OTHER ISSUES

Backstage staff often find themselves dealing with unusual situations that aren't covered in standard reference books. And standard reference books rarely discuss how you train your backstage staff to deal with those situations—assuming you are fortunate enough to always have sufficient staff.

Those who do work back stage have to know how to act during those situations—and at all times, for that matter. Even those who aren't precisely backstage staff—such as the actors—need to follow certain rules of decorum when they are back stage.

We've covered some of the more challenging of these situations in *Stage Directions* over the years, and include them here in this last part of our look at what goes on behind the scenes.

49 | *Where Have All the Techies Gone?*

Working back stage—building sets, hanging lights, doing what needs to be done—is, for many, a joy, something they have trained for or always looked forward to. Admittedly, though, not everyone feels that way. Consequently, for many community theaters in particular it can be difficult to find enough techies to staff a whole season—or even a particular production. If that's your situation, here's some pointed advice.

Create Your Own Talent Pool

As the general manager of one community theater explained, "We are a group in a university town, so we compete for competent stage crews, directors, costumers, etc., with the university theater department, the community parks and recreation program, and another brand-new community theater 14 miles away. How do we replenish our small supply of good techies who keep getting burned out?"

How, indeed? The fact is, this is not an unusual problem in community-based theater companies. Good technical people are always in short supply, and tend to be used again and again. As these people burn out, you recruit new ones, but this becomes more difficult as the talent pool dries up.

The answer is to create your own talent pool through an ongoing training program that has the full support of your board and your current technical staff. There are five components to a good training program: (1) identify specific staffing needs, (2) identify and commit resources, (3) identify potential technical staff for training, (4) train, and (5) assess and refine the process.

1. *Identify staffing needs.* Draw up a list of the staff you need and the skill level required for each. Prioritize the list so you can satisfy the most important needs immediately.

2. *Identify resources.* Next, identify the resources available to develop and implement a training program. What people can you call on, for example, as trainers? (You might find that some of the "burned-out" ones may be willing to give some time to the training effort because they can see that it's going to be a long-term solution. Make it clear to them that you don't expect them to come back as technical staff, that you want their help to create a new generation of techies. You may find that the experience of training new people is so positive that some of the burned-out ones may return to the fold, knowing that now they won't have to shoulder the burden alone.) If no one on staff is available to train, is there someone you can bring in, perhaps from a local college or even another theater company? If you bring in a trainer or decide to send volunteers to a nearby college for instruction, you'll need to support the effort with dollars. Even an in-house training program will have expenses, including materials for workshops. Think of it as an investment in the company's future. One way to cut costs is to purchase and use training videotapes, such as those produced by Theatre Arts Visual Library (800-456-8285).

3. *Identify potential staff.* You may already know volunteers who show potential, or who have expressed an interest, but currently aren't qualified. A good way to identify potential technical staff is to offer entry-level workshops in lighting or set design. Talking with attendees, you can quickly size up who should be encouraged to enter a longer-term training program.

4. *Train.* Training can be either a formal or informal process. A formal training program might include workshops or classes, hands-on experience, and/or apprenticeship. Such a program needs to be well organized and offered on a regular basis over time in order to do any good. Remember, your goal is to create a long-term solution, not just a response to the current shortage of skilled help. Remember, too, that not all technical theater staff are good trainers, and it may be better to send students to a local community college or university for a few classes.

5. *Assess and refine.* The last step is to monitor the program's effectiveness. Ask for feedback from trainers and students, and analyze how your theater company is benefiting from the investment. Then make improvements to the program as needed.

Decent Exposure

If you work back stage, we have news for you: you are not alone. But in addition to your fellow workers, actors, and assorted others, you may have to get used to a new group of backstage people: tourists.

Backstage Tours Can Do Your Company a World of Good—If You Know How

NANCIANNE PFISTER

"Thehe Bonstelle [theater] is supposedly haunted by the ghost of Jessie Bonstelle, so all our tours include a couple of ghost stories," says Wendy Evans of Wayne State University in Detroit.

Even without a resident wraith to show off, your company may be thinking of opening your backstage area to the general public, local students, season-ticket holders, or donors. How does it work? Is it safe? What are the benefits? Hazards?

We asked five theater companies these questions and more: Who gets the tour? What is included? Is it free? Who should conduct it? We also checked with a firm that deals in theatrical insurance. What if a guest trips on a cable? What if someone leans on the rigging or breaks a chair loaned for the current production? The responses we received were informative.

Why Do It?

The reasons for offering tours are diverse. Some just want to make their audiences feel more at home. "It is one of the best opportunities for theatergoers to get an overall feeling for what we do," says Deborah Elliott of the Oregon Shakespeare Festival. "They are allowed into places usually used only by actors, designers, and technicians. It makes our patrons feel special."

Ginny Winsor of Omaha Community Playhouse agrees:

"We offer backstage tours because people always like to feel they are in the know and catch a glimpse of how we do this magic of theater. Getting to see back stage gives them that feeling."

A very different purpose is served by tours that Wayne State provides a group called The Understudies, which raises money for the theater. The tours give them a firmer understanding of the theater so they can answer questions prospective donors may have. Seattle Children's Theatre offers tours to its board members for a similar reason.

On the other hand, Cleveland's Playhouse Square sees its tours for the general public as a promotional tool. As Director of Theater Operations, John Hemsath, told us, "Half of our funding comes directly from the public. This is a chance for them to come to the theater without a ticket." The hope is that, feeling included, they will return to purchase tickets for a future production.

Like most other colleges, Wayne State provides tours of its facility to prospective students. It also includes tours with its student matinee program, as does SCT. "We have a local college that offers a degree in theater administration. It's important for those students to know all the aspects of production," said SCT's Susan O'Connell. "We also give tours to high school theater classes. We may have ten different tours a week."

Omaha Community Playhouse also offers different tours, according to Ginny Winsor, including many for school groups, "but we also try to attract service clubs—Rotary, Kiwanis, etc.—with lunch and tours so they will begin to feel a vested interest in OCP. These clubs and the businesses they represent become strong supporters of our programming."

What to Show

There seems to be general agreement that showing more on the tours is better. In Cleveland, Hemsath says, "Whatever we can show, we do. We begin with a slide show that gives the history of all four theaters—originally vaudeville houses—in Playhouse Square. It goes on to show the years of vacancy and then the restoration process that has been completed in three of the four buildings. The tour takes about two hours."

"For a tour to be educational, it should show how all the elements of a production work together," STC's O'Connell says. "Our tours are limited because our scene shop and costume shop are off-site. Our new onsite tech pavilion will have floor-to-ceiling windows so people can see the more intricate aspects of production."

The tour at Wayne State changes according to the interests of the touring group. If it's another university class, the focus will be related to the course content. After showing the backstage facilities, visitors may be treated to lighting demonstrations or some other area of technical interest.

In Oregon, the 1-hour-and-45-minute tour begins at the Black Swan, the 140-seat arena theater. Tour guides talk about the facility and about the kinds of plays performed in this intimate space. The tour then moves to the Elizabethan outdoor theater. The theater boasts extraordinary acoustics that are demonstrated for visitors as they stand on stage. If their tour guide is an actor, guests may hear some personal stories of what it's like to perform in the rain or to compete with bats, bugs, and the Big Dipper for the attention of the audience. The tour then moves to the six-hundred–seat, state-of-the-art Angus Bomar theater. En route, the group sees the prop-building shop, the green room, dressing rooms, the wig room, and the costume/wardrobe areas.

At the Oregon Shakespeare Festival, which hosts 130 groups each day, tours average twenty to thirty-five people, the same number assigned at SCT. SCT's O'Connell notes that business seems to come in spurts, with a big crowd in March and then almost no one until May.

Tour Guides

If you've ever been trapped with an ineffectual docent or tour guide, you can appreciate the need to train backstage guides. The level of instruction varies from "semi-formalized" at Wayne State to "intensive training" at Oregon Shakespeare Festival. Omaha's volunteers are trained, with a script. No one we talked with allows their guides to wing it.

"Our guides are given basic information, then allowed to personalize it according to their experience and the tour group," said Wendy Evans of Wayne State, adding, "Whether the tour is led by a student, a technician, or a faculty member, we always try to have students around to talk with guests, especially if the guests are prospective students."

At Playhouse Square, training began as a six-hour lecture. As time went by, one volunteer rose to the top and developed a manual with transcripts and an outline. He is now in charge of training and assigning the volunteer guides.

Many Oregon Shakespeare Festival tours are conducted by actors. Stage managers, costume builders, house managers, and other audience service staff also guide visitors. Since guests are encouraged to ask questions, guides must be prepared with a variety of information. "Our tour guides have intensive training," says the Festival's Deborah Elliott. "They have to know the history of the theaters and of the festival. They must know the schedule of the current season, including the directors, designers, and number of performances. They are asked about casting and about our annual budget. They are often asked how many people are involved or what the economic impact on the city is."

Liability

Good hosts are responsible for the safety of their guests. What are the risks of allowing visitors back stage in your theater? Will your liability insurance costs rise when you open your work areas? How do you protect your visitors and your company?

William Haycook is an agent for liability insurance designed for theater companies by Dan Castle of Ponta, Castle, and Ingram Agency. In general, he says, "your cost goes up as your risk goes up, but there is no single answer. Backstage tours are covered in our American Association of Community Theatre insurance program, as such tours are seen as a 'not unforeseen liability risk.' They may be covered by other insurance policies as well, but it is always best to check with your current agent to verify coverage."

While insurance is a good thing, it's a better thing to prevent accidents that would result in a claim. Haycook offers common-sense advice. "As with any liability exposure," he says, "there are things you can do to minimize the risk of injury: use only experienced tour guides, keep all areas well lighted, use glow-tape to show the actual tour route, review tour ground rules with the participants, and clearly mark areas that are off limits to visitors."

SCT's O'Connell agrees: "We have a very controlled tour. Perhaps because we're a children's theater, we're more in tune and aware of the danger zones. We have what we call our "kid patrol" to keep people from wandering into places they should not be. We make sure every place is safe to walk through."

There is little question that backstage tours are good public relations, whether to reward volunteers, show need to potential donors, or just give your patrons a sense of inclusion. Whether your company offers such a tour depends on what benefits you might derive from it. One thing seems certain: The success of the tour lies in the hands of the tour guides. They must be informed, enthusiastic, and prepared for anything. Even a ghost.

51 | *On Your Best Behavior*

In the Dressing Room, Green Room, or Elsewhere, Keep the Focus on the Show Itself

STEPHEN PEITHMAN

*E*tiquette, the dictionary says, refers to "the forms and manners established by convention as acceptable or required in social relations or profession." Luckily, the rules of theatrical etiquette spring from one simple concern—to avoid anything that might impair or weaken the performance. With this in mind, let's take a look at the etiquette of the dressing room, green room, and other backstage areas.

No Visitors, Please

Concentration, writes Doug Moston in his book, *Coming to Terms with Acting* (Drama Books), is the "ability or act of focusing all your attention or energy where you want or need it." Thus, anything that interferes with actors' concentration can damage their performance—and the show. That is why people not involved in the production must not be allowed backstage until after the performance. Visitors, even well intentioned, are at best a needless distraction and at worst a downright nuisance.

A note in the program and a large sign at the backstage door take care of the majority of would-be visitors. There are others, however, who may demand special attention. For example, a "No Visitors" sign is sometimes ignored by company members who aren't in the current production, but who feel free to come back stage because they consider themselves "a member of the family."

The truth is, each production develops its own sense of

family, a dynamic that can be compromised by even a friendly outsider. Any backstage visitor either must be greeted or ignored, and either way that takes some energy on the part of the actors who are preparing for the show.

Akin to the "we're not visitors—we're family" ploy is the cast or crew member who brings along a child. Of course, emergency situations do arise (the sitter doesn't show up), but in general, children who are not part of the production do not belong in the green room or dressing room. They quickly grow bored and get underfoot and in the way. They may pose a danger to themselves or others. And when their parent is on stage or helping with the set, they either go unsupervised or divert the energy of cast and crew members. Forget the "you won't even know they're here" ploy—you most assuredly will.

Keep It Down

Einstein once said energy can neither be created nor destroyed. That is not true back stage, however. Here energy *is* created—both the positive, focused kind that helps drive the performance, and the negative kind produced by such simple but often overlooked stressors as noise.

Therefore, radios or stereos don't belong. Let's face it—it's almost impossible to find music that *everybody* likes, so it's bound to bother someone. In addition, simple conversation has to compete with the sound level of actors speaking louder or straining to be heard. More important, ambient noise can obscure important communication—such as the stage manager's warning of "Places, please!"

By the same token, it's wise to ask that actors keep their voices down and save their energy for the stage. Those who do vocal warmups should go into the restroom or outside. However, there is one important exception: if the cast does vocal warmups as a group, the focus on the performance is maintained and strengthened.

Stay Focused

During the show, card games and the like can help pass the time, but unless you're doing one of those big shows where the ensemble has 20 minutes or more between entrances, actors are usually better off conserving their energy and focusing on their next entrance. Card games also may lead to loud conversations that can fray the voice, and in some cases, even can be heard from the house.

I have noticed a great deal less of this kind of thing with one theater company I work with. The reason: a video monitor has been installed and the cast can watch the show from the green room. This not only keeps the actors more focused on the progress of the show, but reduces the number of people watching from the wings.

Respect Their Space

It is, of course, simple courtesy not to shove others' clothes or personal items out of the way to make room for your own. If there is a shortage of space, the stage manager should call everyone together to brainstorm a mutually acceptable solution.

Respecting others' space also means that actors need to clean up after themselves. Dealing with another person's mess is unneccesarily stress-inducing and can affect the quality of a performance—and that can affect everyone in the show.

Respect others' mental space as well. For example, some actors prefer to be quiet before a performance. Be sensitive to this and don't try to strike up a conversation. The great Italian actress Anna Magnani, whose emotional vitality was never in need of stimulation, used to work alone on a crossword puzzle before every performance. She did so, she said, because it was her *mind* that needed waking up.

Keep Your Cool

An actress in heavy conversation in the dressing room did not hear her cue and was seriously late for an entrance. By not paying attention, she caused the show to stumble and created momentary panic among the other performers. That was problem enough, but the situation was compounded when she was bawled out as soon as she left the stage. Her subsequent performance was overheated and out of control as she worked off her anger.

While it may seem logical to deal with bad behavior immediately, it's better for the show if you wait until after the final curtain. You'll be in control of your temper and will have had time to phrase your comments to best advantage. (In this case, a chewing out was probably unnecessary. The actress in question was well aware of her transgression and its effect on her fellow actors.)

Don't Move It

"I came backstage to make a quick change," recalls one actor, "and my costume wasn't where I'd left it before the show started. I broke into a sweat, I panicked. I hunted for my costume for several minutes, and with my dresser's help finally found it—on another rack where someone had moved it without telling me. I barely made my change in time, and when I walked out onto the stage I was still jittery and—well, I stunk."

Thus this simple rule: Don't move anything belonging to someone else without permission. Actors must be confident that when they look for a costume or reach for a prop they have placed off stage, it will be there. The moment of panic may be brief, but who needs it?

I once shared a hat with another actor. I wore the hat in Act I, he wore it in Act II. My head being larger than his, at final dress rehearsal he stuck paper toweling in the lining around the brim so it would fit better. However, he didn't tell me what he had done and I didn't notice the padding when I put it on and walked on stage opening night. I was baffled as the hat mysteriously refused to stay on my head. It rattled me and I—well, I stunk.

Button It Up

"Guess who's going to be in the house tonight?" an actor yelled as he came in the green-room door. The celebrity was a well-known local director, and you can imagine how the news of his presence affected some of the performers. One forgot her lines; another actually padded his part.

Ask the cast not to discuss who's in the audience and certainly not to scan the audience for familiar faces to share with the others. The actor's focus should be on what's happening on stage, not out in the house.

Back stage also is not a group therapy session. Actors need to remember their personal lives are just that—personal. There are always exceptions, of course; sometimes a traumatic event must be acknowledged. For the most part, however, it's best to leave one's troubles outside. Psychiatrists often encourage patients to become other-directed, to move beyond the preoccupation with self. How better to do that than in the ensemble environment of the theater?

The Golden Rule

Probably the best advice regarding backstage etiquette is simply to practice the Golden Rule: treat others as you want to be treated and keep in mind why you're there.

Allowing the actor to focus on the performance is at the heart of these backstage rules of behavior. After all, the actors *are* the performance.

52 | *It Seemed Like a Good Idea at the Time*

We've spent much of this book offering instruction on how to do things right when you're back stage so that, of course, the performance can be the best it can be. But, inevitably, things do go wrong—back stage and, ultimately, on stage as well. The good news is that sometimes we can learn just as much from what goes wrong—and we can do it while we're laughing.

Theatrical Disaster Stories Are Funny—and Can Be Instructive

*L*aughter and applause greeted Lady Bracknell on her first entrance in a production of *The Importance of Being Earnest*. And no wonder. Outfitted in a stern, tailored suit of velvet and satin, her head was crowned by an oversized hat on which perched a bird of prey, wings outstretched, as though ready to attack.

However, by the second performance it was obvious to anyone with a sense of smell that the bird had never received the services of a taxidermist. After the Sunday matinee the head fell off and had to be repositioned with pins, and the hat was refrigerated between performances. However, that did not eliminate the general odor of decay—nor the discomfort of the actress playing Lady Bracknell—although her understandably sour look added immeasurably to her characterization.

Here at *Stage Directions*, we've heard lots of horror stories like these, but haven't used them much in articles. After all, we are a how-to magazine. However, after hearing several recent examples of what we call "it seemed like a good idea at the time" stories, we've decided there is a lesson here: when trying something new, think through all the possible results of your actions. And remember, Murphy's Law reigns supreme.

Going to Seed

The costumer who produced Lady Bracknell's hat was a novice, but even experienced designers have their share of embarrassments.

"When designing a fat suit to beef up a slender actress, realism was our prime concern," recalls one experienced and understandably anonymous costumer. "There was a great deal of discussion and testing of what to stuff the prosthetic breasts with. Finally, we decided to go with birdseed. It is inexpensive and looks and moves very naturally. After several hot, sweaty performances, however, the seeds began to germinate and the seam in one 'breast' gave way during a performance, spilling its contents onto the actress and the floor."

And, we assume, stopping the show.

The Grass Is Greener

Using untried materials can cause problems for just about anyone. Lighting consultant Gregory Despopoulos recalls a director who demanded the stage floor be laid with real sod. To protect the floor, the theater tech used sheets of heavy-gauge plastic, carefully overlapped, then covered with dirt. Finally, a professional lawn company installed grass sod on top. The grass, of course, had to be watered and given enough light during the day to prevent it from turning yellow. But the real problem became clear after the set was struck. While the plastic had been overlapped, the seams had not been sealed, and water seeped through. The entire stage floor had to be replaced.

Keep It Simple

Charles Myler, who not long ago retired from St. Mary's University in San Antonio, Texas, recalls a period during which he became very experimental. "I got the bright idea of doing *The Petrified Forest* as expressionistic—like Elmer Rice's *The Adding Machine*. The walls were incomplete, the doors were slanted and the windows were hanging in space. The actors were going to be as stylized as possible and entrances were to be made through the audience. It was a major failure.

The realistic dialogue fought with the visual set. The actors had no idea what I was trying to accomplish and the audience was completely confused. After this fiasco, I did *Inherit the Wind* as it should be done—realistic."

Out and About

Mark Brownell of Toronto recalls a production of *Cowboy Mouth*, staged in a Toronto pub. The director decided that what was needed was an impromptu improvisation from her two actors to stimulate the creative juices for the production. One of the actors pulled a starter's pistol and proceeded to kidnap the other actor in full view of the bar's patrons. A nervous barmaid phoned the cops and a squadron of police showed up outside the bar with guns drawn ready to fire. After a few terrifying moments the actors were arrested and eventually charged with mischief. The director, Brownell reports, was not charged.

Crickets Are Calling

Allowing enough time is frequently the cause of theatrical disasters, large or small. For a production of *Suddenly, Last Summer*, background sound effects of a midsummer evening, complete with cricket calls, were used. This was not only effective for the audience, but also attracted large numbers of crickets into the theater.

"We didn't use the tape until the first preview performance," admitted an embarrassed soundman. "If we had tried it earlier we could have corrected the problem, maybe even sprayed. But once the crickets got in, they didn't leave. They certainly sounded realistic, but we couldn't turn them off, either."

Not trying things out in advance caused grief for Kate Bolgrien, who was technical director of a production of *Deathtrap*, whose script calls for a thunderstorm. "I wasn't happy with any of the sound effects that I tried during tech rehearsals, so the afternoon of the final preview I went shopping again and found what I thought would be the perfect tape, called *Country Thunderstorm*. I listened to the first couple of minutes and it sounded perfect, just the right mix of rain and thunder, a nice build to the storm. During the performance, everything was going fine, the storm sounded great, when I started to hear sheep. Yes, *sheep*. And eventually goats, cows, and chickens. Apparently, the country thunderstorm included livestock! The audience could only speculate as to why these two men were keeping sheep on the premises—and why they sounded frightened."

Ka-Boom!

In *You Can't Take It with You*, Paul is supposed to light a firecracker he has made. The community-theater company wasn't allowed to use the real thing on stage without a pyrotechnic expert, which it couldn't afford. So the firecracker was defused and the actor playing Paul would pretend to light it with a match while an offstage starting pistol made the bang. To hide the fact that the firecracker did not really explode, the actor carried it on stage in a cast-iron frying pan. Removing the fuse is no protection from a lighted match, however, and the resulting explosion not only startled the actor, but also deafened him for the next few minutes.

If a small explosion can be dangerous, consider the effect of a large one. Recalls Brian Oberquell of Olympia, Washington: "I was asked to design and implement the special effects for a play in which a woodstove explodes (noise, smoke, and a flying top) when an actor pours gas on the wood and throws in a match. I was trying to figure out methods ranging from trip levers to compressed air when the technical director told me he'd made a steel mortar for me to use; a small powder charge would provide the smoke, noise, and enough force to make the stove lid pop up. The mortar itself was a work of art that I had no qualms about using. However, I was *very* reluctant to put this into an enclosed area like a stove (not to mention inside a theater) without running a number of outdoor tests first.

"The TD and I set the mortar up in the front yard of the theater, and I put an electric igniter in for the powder. The TD put in a 'palm-full' of black powder (I felt it was too much but hey, it was his mortar . . . and this *was* a test) and set the stove lid on top. We retired to a safe distance and I ignited the powder. Judging from the 'hang time' of the cast-iron stove lid, we guessed that it went up about 150 feet . . . and when it came down it landed on a concrete walkway, shattering into a number of pieces. I sent the TD off to weld the lid together, and I went home and designed a system that involved triggering a trip lever that hit the lid and caused it to pop up—an effect that was safe, effective (judging from the shouts and gasps of surprise from the audience), and guaranteed to leave the lights and ceiling of the theater intact."

And the actors and audience intact, as well.

The Minerva Effect

And finally, there is the tale of Jim Mica of Ithaca, New York, centering around a production of Gilbert & Sullivan's *Princess Ida*. In the second act of this lesser G&S effort, Ida sings a hymn to the goddess

Minerva. For this, the set designer provided a statue of the goddess, who stood 4 feet high and poured water from a jug on her hip.

"She stood on a platform with a kid's wading pool—cleverly disguised as a marble pond—on a lower platform in front of her," Mica recalls. "The first pumping effort ended in failure when the set designer learned that a pump rated to raise water 2 feet will not raise it 4 feet, even when the water is for a fountain in an imaginary castle. We got a heftier pump. It worked: Minerva now produced a very audible sound of tinkling water."

Princess Ida is in three acts—the second, in which the fountain made its first appearance, runs a little more than an hour. "When we closed the curtain on the second act there was a stampede for the bathrooms," Mica says. "Our ushers tried to stem the tide by blocking the side exits and telling everybody to stay near their seats because this was to be a very brief intermission. There were, thankfully, no injuries or accidents."

The Minerva Effect continued throughout the run of the play and eventually hit the cast and crew as well.

"During the third performance one of the assistant stage managers called me to her station, ripped off her headset, and hissed 'I've got to go!' During the final performance, just before the second-act curtain, I came upon one of the principals behind the farthest upstage flat doing what Gilbert might have described as a Micturition Minuet. She looked at me with anguish in her eyes and whispered loudly, 'That *statue*!' "

Finders Keepers

To attract more backstage help, the Chippewa Valley Theatre Guild, in Eau Claire, Wisconsin, offers workshops it calls "Discovery Days" on two successive Saturdays each year. On the first Saturday, attendees meet and talk with several of CVTG's veteran technicians and other volunteers in the scene shop, enjoy a light continental breakfast, and choose three areas of interest for the day—sound, lighting, props, costumes, hair and makeup, scenery, stage tech, and auditioning. Each session lasts 45 minutes and includes an overview of the activities and responsibilities of each area. Attendees receive hands-on experience in running lights, preparing props, building scenery, or altering a costume. On the second Saturday, attendees choose one area of interest from day one and spend a full morning learning the specifics of that area under the guidance of veteran technical staff and volunteers.

Tech Vest

Sporting vests are designed for outdoors activities, but could be useful for scenic designers and other technical folk who need to carry important items with them while they work. Made of cotton blend, a typical vest has six outside pockets, two inside pockets, and a deep backpack pouch. These are available from many outlets in standard canvas color.

PMS Day

Washington State's Whidby Playhouse has declared the first Saturday of each month as PMS Day. In this case, "PMS" stands for Preventive Maintenance Saturday. "Whatever projects need doing will be addressed starting at 9 A.M. on these days," announces the company newsletter. "We'll spruce the place up and catch any little problems before they become big problems."

Watch It

When using familiar household items for backstage use, be careful to make their new use obvious. Reports Mike Bromberg of the Sudbury [New Hampshire] Savoyards, one of the lighting crew had used a large plastic garbage can to carry cables to the auditorium where a company dinner was to be held. "Several cables and two-fers were still in the bin when someone commandeered it (without looking inside) as a trash can for dinner garbage," Bromberg says. "We found the cables at the bottom of much gummy foodstuff, and we had to wash the cables and hang them up to dry."

Volunteer Aid

Make available a glossary of your company's particular jargon and slang for volunteers and new members. This helps them more quickly understand memos, discussions, and special projects. And the next time you're explaining a job to a new volunteer or staff person, ask them to take thorough notes on the procedures for each task. Then have them type up their notes to include in a looseleaf binder. Not only will the new staff person learn, but you will be building a permanent procedures manual for others to follow. Be sure to make a photocopy so you can review the procedures at your leisure.

"Next Time" File

You might suggest that your production people start a "next time" file. Put all materials and information about a specific task in a separate folder, then put a piece of bright colored paper at the front of the folder on which you jot notes about what could be done better next time you have the same responsibility.

For All to See

Consider covering one wall back stage or in the green room with cork. This permits any part of the wall to be used as a bulletin board and helps prevent the scarring of plasterboard or paneled walls. The cork is also sound-absorbent, and can cut down on backstage noise.

Final Words

"Great art conceals art," said Konstantin Stanislavski, the great drama teacher and developer of Method acting. He was referring to actors who are believable in their roles because they don't seem to be acting. They make us believe that they are the characters they are playing, and that everything they say and do is happening spontaneously as we watch.

Great art does conceal art, and not only the art of the actor; the illusion of reality presented by a play is dependent upon the design and technical elements of the production as well. The actor, director, and technical staff work as a team to create the delicate illusionary reality that we call theater. A great performance doesn't simply happen; it is the result of planning, talent, dedication, and teamwork.

We hope this book has been helpful as you work as part of the backstage team.

Contributors

MIKE BROMBERG is a regular contributor to *Stage Directions*. He is an electronic design engineer who designs lighting principally for light opera in the New England area.

ELBIN CLEVELAND is a professor of scenic design and technology at the University of South Carolina.

EILEEN P. DUGGAN is editor of a community newspaper in St. Louis, a freelance music critic, and has served as a dresser and seamstress for several theater groups.

KATHLEEN GRIFFIN is marketing director with I. Weiss & Sons, Inc., a New York supplier of stage draperies and rigging, established in 1900.

GEORGE F. LEDO is an architectural-space planning consultant who has worked for many years in repertory, summer stock, and community theater.

STEPHEN PEITHMAN is co-founder of *Stage Directions*, where he served as Editor-in-Chief for eleven years. He is currently Consulting Editor at the magazine.

NANCIANNE PFISTER, former Associate Editor of *Stage Directions*, teaches at American River College in Sacramento, California.

BILL SAPSIS is president of Sapsis Rigging, Inc., and has been working in the theater professionally for more than twenty years.